WOMEN OF THE
IRISH RISING:
A PEOPLE'S HISTORY

WOMEN OF THE IRISH RISING: A PEOPLE'S HISTORY

Michael Hogan

Asociación Internacional de Historia Militar A.C.

FONDO EDITORIAL UNIVERSITARIO

Fondo Editorial Universitario
Guadalajara, Jalisco, México

Publisher's Cataloguing-In-Publication Date
Name: Hogan, Michael 1943-
Title: *Women of the Irish Rising: A People's History*
Michael Hogan

Interior design by: Ediciones de la Noche
Cover design by: Ana Maria Calatayud.

Includes bibliographical references and index.
Cover image. Constance Markiewicz. 1916. National Museum of Ireland.

ISBN: 978-84-18791-30-7

Subject: Easter Rising 1916, Irish War of Independence-1919-1921, Irish 20th century history, Irish literature, Irish Constitution of 1937, women's rights in Ireland, feminism-history, intersectional feminism, socialism, World War I-1916-1919, US-Ireland foreign relations, conflict studies, Connolly, James (1868-1916), Skinnider, Margaret (1893-1971), Markiewicz, Constance (1868-1971), Lynn, Kathleen (1874-1955).

Published simultaneously in the US and Mexico by Fondo Editorial Universitario in cooperation with the Asociación Internacional de Historia Militar, A.C., and the Sociedad Mexicana de Geografía y Estadísticas de Jalisco.

When the history of this fight is written, the foremost page in the annals should be given to the women of Dublin who had taken their place in the fight for the establishment of the republic.

Pádraic Pearse

TABLE OF CONTENTS

DEDICATION

In loving memory of my maternal grandfather Cornelius Mc-Gillicuddy (1884-1965) with gratitude for instilling in me a love of Irish history, and my grandmother Annie Keane McGillicuddy (1887-1916) whom I only knew in stories because she died too young.

AUTHOR'S NOTE

T here are several truly excellent books about the Irish Rising of 1916. Most of them provide clear insights into the causes of the revolt, accounts of the battles, the surrender to overwhelming odds, the executions, and repercussions. Yet, when I speak to young people in the US and Latin America, I find that they know little about this period of Irish history. For the young women in my world history classes both in the US and in Mexico, this is often coupled with indifference.

In the US there are 32 million people who claim Irish descent. Another 4.5 million in Canada, and 500,000 in Argentina. In Mexico there was an Irish Battalion[1] which fought gallantly to preserve Mexican freedom. They are still remembered today in street names and monuments. But again, very little is known by the young people in Mexico or other countries in the Americas about the history of the Irish people themselves and their own struggle for freedom. The handful of books that mention women in the Rising are largely academic and presume a basic knowledge of Irish history and the events of the Rising itself.

In 1995 I took my daughter, Melissa Field (née Hogan) Wiley, on a tour of Ireland and she was fascinated. We did a historical walk around the center of Dublin where most of the action during the Rising took place. We visited the General Post Office, St. Stephen's Green, Dublin Castle, City Hall, the Shelbourne Hotel, and of course, the Kilmainham Gaol where the captured rebels were imprisoned and then executed. We saw a statue memorializing Constance Markiewicz, who trained many young soldiers and fought with the Irish Citizen Army, and a plaque honoring Margaret Skin-

---

[1] Michael Hogan, *The Irish Soldiers of Mexico* (Guadalajara: Fondo Editorial Universitario, 1997).

nider, who was shot three times by British soldiers as she attempted to rush a fortified position.

Melissa was so moved by the things she saw and the history she learned in the days and months that followed, that she wrote her senior thesis at the University of Colorado on the more recent Irish conflict which she easily traced to unresolved issues from the past. She sent a copy to former president Bill Clinton. He was so impressed by her thesis that he hired her to work with his team on the Good Friday Agreement of 1998 which finally brought a semblance of peace to Northern Ireland. Melissa's work was primarily with women, both Protestant and Catholic, whose children were directly affected by the violence. It was these women who used their combined moral force to bring the Sinn Fein and the Unionists to the bargaining table.

My grandfather Cornelius McGillicuddy, to whom this book is dedicated, was born in Cahersiveen, County Kerry, in 1883. He was 33 at the time of the Easter Rising. His wife, Annie Keane McGillicuddy, who died in 1916, was only 29. He spoke to me often of the sacrifices the women of the Rising made, and how important they were to the cause although their contributions continued to be neglected by historians. For many years I searched for more stories about these women. I read journals, diaries, some wonderful articles in the *Irish Times*, *RTE*, *Irish History*, and the Sinn Fein archives. In addition, over the past few years, I discovered some excellent biographies of some of the women who participated in the Rising, as well as books which approached the Rising through a feminist lens and attempted to give the reader a broader picture.[2] What I did not find (and the reason for this book) was an accessible

---

[2]   Among the many fine biographies, I would include Anne Clare's *Unlikely Rebels: The Gifford Girls and the Fight for Irish Freedom*; Margaret Ward's *Fearless Woman: Hanna Sheehy Skeffington*, and Margaret O'Hogartaigh's *Kathleen Lynn: Irishwoman, Patriot, Doctor*. Books which more fully sketch out the participation of women in the Rising would include Linda Connolly's *Women and the Irish Revolution: Feminism, Activism, Violence*; Ruth Taillon's *The Women of 1916*, and Ann Matthews' *Renegades: Irish Republican Women 1910-1922*. As mentioned, these are books written by academics for a scholarly audience. In fact, the Matthews book was based on her PhD dissertation.

Fig. 1 Melissa Field (née Hogan) Wiley and former US president Bill Clinton. Dublin, 1998.

and compelling narrative of the Rising which preserved the drama and contradictory elements of the struggle and integrated the activities of the women as part of a seamless whole. What I did not find was how the ideals of these women and men, like the rebel leader James Connolly, were put to the test in the years that followed. Nor did I find any testament to how those ideals continue to be relevant today as the multinational corporations and spineless politicians which replaced the neocolonial exploitation of working men and women sell the birthright of the citizens to the Commons.

What Connolly knew, and women rebel leaders such as Margaret Skinnider and Constance Markiewicz knew, is that the Rising would have been futile if the Irish people managed merely to replace one master with another. They all knew that compromise with the unlimited growth of corporate power would be the beginning of wage feudalism. What they also understood was that the free press, once so respected, had become embedded in the pockets of its advertisers and would promote their interests rather than that of the ordinary citizens.

The resulting book, I believe, will be read by students in the Americas who can approach it on several levels. For younger students it might be just a great adventure story, in which women share the stage with men. For others, it will provide their first insights into the fascinating complexities of Irish history. For even more thoughtful students, it might be seen as a history that shows the persistence of ideas such as socialism (much disparaged by conservatives in the US and elsewhere). As economic insecurity, destruction of the environment, and sale of public utilities undermine the very meaning of homeland, Connolly's words still ring true:

> If you remove the English army to-morrow and hoist the green flag over Dublin Castle, unless you set about the organization of the Socialist Republic your efforts would be in vain...the green-coated Irish soldiers will guard the fraudulent gains of capitalist and landlord from 'the thin hands of the poor' just as remorselessly and just as effectually as the scarlet-coated emissaries of England do today.[3]

So, this book is an attempt to remedy that insufficiency as well as to provide a small legacy for my daughter. While the book strives for historical accuracy and provides careful research and documentation, it also attempts to craft an arresting narrative to capture the interest of young people, especially young women. It is my hope that by understanding the courage and sacrifice of those who fought for freedom and human rights, they will see that they are not alone but stand on the shoulders of rugged feminists (not only

---

[3] Peter Beresford Ellis (ed.), *James Connolly - Selected Writings* (London: Pluto Press, 1988), 124.

Fig. 2 Annie (Keane) and Cornelius McGillicuddy. Watertown, County Kerry, 1913.

women, but thoughtful men as well) who have gone before them.
All personal insights and observations of the women recounted
here are from primary sources such as journals, letters of the period, and interviews of participants. The descriptions of battles,
the day-to-day timeline, and the general history of the Rising have
been gleaned from newspaper reports, military documents, and
commentaries of careful historians whose care and learning I cannot hope to replicate, but to whom I have given credit and whose
contributions have been documented along the way.

1

THE BEST OF YEARS,
THE WORST OF YEARS

E aster, 1916. It seemed like the perfect time to wage a rebellion against British rule. Their troops were fully occupied on the Continent fighting Germany in the trenches. Those left behind to guard their Irish possessions were few and ill-prepared. Plus, Easter had a symbolic meaning for all Christians. Just as Christ rose from the dead, so would the Irish rise up from 400 years of oppression and take possession of their land and their culture once more.

On the other hand, a bill had been introduced in Parliament to offer Home Rule to the Irish which would give them a measure of autonomy without a revolution.

The problem was that the Unionists in the North were totally against home rule because it would put the Catholic majority in control. In addition, they had formed their own civilian army to fight if such a bill were passed.

Conversely, since the British allowed the Unionists to form their own civilian army called the Ulster Volunteers,[4] they could hardly object to those in the South forming their paramilitary group, the Irish Volunteers, to defend themselves. This group, along with another called the Irish Citizen Army that would come mainly from the workers' unions, would form the core of the Irish rebellion and with proper arms could perhaps overthrow their British rulers.

The problem was that they had insufficient arms and were dependent on shipments from abroad. The Germans were willing

---

[4] Charles Townshend, *Easter 1916: The Irish Rebellion* (London: Kindle edition, 2006), 1-10.

to supply such arms, but anyone caught smuggling German arms could be charged with treason and hanged.

There were groups of all sorts in favor of an uprising. The workers and trade unionists because they had suffered under the oppressive paternalism of British owners who controlled the police and brutally put down strikes. The humanists and scholars (Gaelic League) because they saw the replacement of Irish language and culture by the English as a destruction of their heritage. The Catholics because they saw the imposition of a Protestant hegemony placing restrictions on their civil rights. And finally, the socialists who saw capitalism as the root of all the troubles. The problem was that each of these groups had different leaders with different agendas.

Meanwhile, ordinary men and women were just going about their daily business trying to get along, make ends meet, and live peaceful lives. Also, since most of the planning was going on in secret, only a select group of citizens even knew that a revolution was brewing. Could there really be a revolution if no one showed up?

Still, 1916 was a good year. Women's rights were coming of age and there were several female leaders already in the forefront. The British Empire was overextended with colonies around the world and a major war was draining resources and manpower. In addition, the massive immigration to the US and Canada during the famine years ensured that there were millions of Irish American sympathizers living abroad who would financially support the cause.

Nevertheless, because Britain had possessions and dependents abroad it could call on them to fill the ranks of its armies. Thus, there were Indian soldiers, Canadian soldiers, New Zealand soldiers, Australian soldiers and, yes, more than 200,000 Irish soldiers who served the Union Jack. In addition, the American government considered England its staunchest ally and as the war progressed President Woodrow Wilson could hardly be sympathetic to any uprising which weakened England's fight against Germany in "the War to make the world safe for democracy."

Yes, 1916 was the perfect year. Perfectly confusing, perfectly complex. The spirit of revolution would rise and ebb, like the fortunes of World War I itself. It would be full of passion and energy but also blunders and foolishness. The spirit of revolt and its forces would rise, then ebb, then rise again. When the smoke cleared from the awful shelling of the British artillery, it would appear a disaster for the Irish, with a bombed-out capital, her leaders hanged as traitors, civilians ruthlessly murdered, women imprisoned, and the boot of the oppressor firmly on the throat of the Irish people. Yet, in a few short years, the tide would change again, and what had appeared to be feckless would be seen as visionary, what had been perceived as disaster would be known as glorious. The Easter Rising of 1916. And the women? Ah, the women. They helped to turn that tide.

Reading the traditional accounts of the period, one would conclude that women played only a minor role in the Rising. Even the most generous of historians assign them roles as messengers and nurses, non-combatants who played no part in the actual planning, were not involved in military operations, and were assigned to secondary roles because of their gender. The two exceptions made are Constance Markiewicz and Margaret Skinnider, whose contributions would be hard to ignore. Markiewicz was, in fact, a leader in the Irish Citizen Army. She not only designed their uniforms and wrote their anthem, but she helped train young troopers, and was armed with an automatic pistol which she used to considerable effect in the various encounters with police and British soldiers in and around St. Stephen's Green. That she ultimately went on to be the first woman elected from Ireland to the House of Commons secured her a place in history, as did the fact that, as a Sinn Fein member, she refused to take her seat after being elected.

Margaret Skinnider wrote a widely read book about her experiences in the Irish Citizen Army both as a sharpshooter and a fearsome sniper. She was also an explosives expert who risked her life on many occasions, in the transport of highly volatile chemicals and fuses, as well as the setting of explosives in houses occupied by British forces. Moreover, during one particular raid she was ambushed at the entrance to a house in which British soldiers were barricaded and was shot three times. All three hits were with "dum

dum" bullets which caused significant and potentially fatal wounds. She survived, not only to tell her story, but to promote Irish nationalism and women's rights for many years thereafter.

However, what is often ignored or glimpsed only in piecemeal articles and not part of the general scheme of things, is the vital role women played in the planning of the Rising and the financing and acquisition of arms without which the Rising would have never taken place. In addition to Markiewicz and Skinnider, there were a host of women noted for their courage and poise under fire who served as quartermasters of the rebels, providing them with food, ammunition, and medicines. Others worked as medical personnel not only as nurses, but also in one case as a surgeon operating under combat conditions. Finally, it was a woman who handled the tricky negotiations with the British general to obtain a ceasefire to save civilian lives and (against her wishes) ultimately delivered the surrender agreement at the request of the Commander-in-Chief Pádraic Pearse.

2

PRELUDE TO WAR 1912-1915

THE CURRAGH INCIDENT: THE ULSTER UNIONISTS ARISE

In 1912, a Home Bill for Ireland was introduced in Parliament by the then-liberal British government of H.H. Asquith. It was to give Ireland some measure of autonomy in deciding its own affairs. Almost immediately the Unionists in Northern Ireland objected to the idea of being governed by a Catholic government in Dublin. That same year they founded the Ulster Volunteers which was basically a paramilitary group dedicated to opposing any attempt to enforce the Home Rule government. A significant number of British senior officers joined the group.

In 1913, General John French, Chief of the Imperial General Staff, warned that if the British army were called upon to enforce the Home Rule bill, and act against the Ulster Volunteers, there might be a split with several officers and their men choosing to fight to preserve the Protestant Imperial government in Ireland. The Army command received reports that the Ulster Volunteers now numbered over 100,000 and were pursuing ways to acquire arms. It was believed that they were planning a raid on the armory at Carrickfergus Castle. General French supported a mission to Northern Ireland to put down the Unionists by force, if necessary. Accordingly, he ordered General Sir Arthur Paget to commence operations against Northern Ireland. Paget met with his officers, and on the evening of March 30 became aware that many of his officers would resign rather than fight against fellow Ulstermen.

Faced with mass resignations and perhaps a mutiny at the Curragh Camp in County Kildare where the main Royal forces were located, the government backed down. Keep in mind that this was the same government which approved the use of force against the Irish trying to organize the workers for better wages during the Dublin lockout[5] where beatings and shootings injured and killed innocent civilians including a 16-year-old girl.[6] Needless to say, the Irish Republican Brotherhood (IRB) was outraged. It was apparent now to the nationalists that they could not expect any support from the British army in Ireland and that they needed to recruit more men to their own paramilitary forces and arm them accordingly.

Less than a month later, the Ulster Volunteers covertly landed 25,000 rifles and between 3 and 5 million rounds of ammunition from the German Empire. Known as the Larne Gun-running Incident, it was the first time that motor vehicles were used on a large scale for military purposes, in this case moving the weapons from the coast to other locations throughout the North. The Ulster forces were led by Major Frederick H. Crawford using his army connections. Crawford was strongly opposed to Home Rule and supported armed resistance in opposing it. His advocation for armed resistance was evident when he remarked at one meeting of the Ulster Volunteers Council that his heart rejoiced when he heard talk of using physical force. At another meeting he went as far as asking some attendees to step into another room where he showed them fixed bayonets, rifles, and cartridges laid out for ready action.

Crawford had tried several times to smuggle arms into Ulster, but vigilant customs officials seized most of them at the docks. However, this time he was successful, landing the shipments in Larne, Donaghadee, and Bangor in the early hours between Friday and Saturday, April 24-25, 1914. The Ulster forces were now armed and ready.

[5] On August 31, 1913, the Dublin Metropolitan Police attacked a union meeting on Sackville Street that had been publicly banned. Over 300 were injured and two were killed in the initial attack. The event is remembered as Bloody Sunday, a term used again after January 30, 1972 when, in the Bogside area of Derry, Northern Ireland, British soldiers shot 26 civilians.

[6] Later that day, Alice Brady, a 16-year-old, was shot dead by a strike-breaker as she brought home a food parcel from the union office. Michael Byrne, a union official, died after being tortured in a police cell. See Alan MacSimoin, "The Dublin Lockout of 1913" (http://www.anarkismo.net/article/470, accessed Dec. 5, 2020).

THE IRISH VOLUNTEERS RESPOND

When the Curragh incident became known, most of the supporters of Home Rule became convinced that only an uprising would do. At the very least the working men and women of the south needed to protect their interests against the Unionists to the north by raising funds to buy arms for the Irish Volunteers. When Pádraic Pearse, senior member of the Volunteers, learned of the Larne shipments, he remarked, "The only thing more ridiculous than an Ulsterman with a rifle is a Nationalist without one."

A group of Irish nationalists began brainstorming ways in which they could raise funds to purchase military grade weapons from Germany. The major players in the operation were Michael O'Rahilly, Sir Roger Casement, Mary Spring Rice, Alice Stopford Green, Darrell Figgis, along with Erskine and Molly Childers.

Casement asked Alice Stopford Green for a loan to be repaid when the Volunteers bought their rifles. Alice was the daughter of the Rector of Kells and Archbishop of Meath; her grandfather was a Church of Ireland bishop. She had married the historian John Richard Green who died six years after their marriage. Alice assumed the burden of his legacy and became a notable historian herself. Stopford Green published her first book on British history in 1888 and a major work on Irish history and culture, *The Making of Ireland and its Undoing*, in 1908. She was also an ardent nationalist.

Meanwhile, Mary Spring Rice and Molly Childers established a fundraising committee, which successfully raised over £2,000. This was a significant amount. It would be the equivalent of £240,000 in today's currency. More than enough to buy a respectable number of rifles and millions of rounds of ammunition.

Casement, Figgis, and Erskine Childers then visited the London agent of a Belgian arms dealer. They eventually closed with a dealer in Hamburg, introduced to them by Michael O'Rahilly, Director of Arms for the Irish Volunteers, and settled on a sale of 1,500 rifles and 49,000 rounds of ammunition. Arrangements were made for the shipment to be delivered at sea. It was understood by

THE CAMERON STUDIO, 70, MORTIMER ST., REGENT STREET.

Fig. 3 Alice Stopford Green, ca. 1888.

the seller that these guns were not to be used in Europe but were to be transshipped to Mexico for use in the Revolution (1910-20) currently in progress.

3

MOLLY CHILDERS
AND THE GUN-RUNNERS

Affectionately called "Molly" from an early age, Mary Alden Osgood Childers was the younger daughter of Dr. Hamilton Osgood and Margaret Cushing Osgood. Born in Boston in 1875 she was raised in wealth and privilege in the exclusive district of Beacon Hill. Indeed, the family's address at 8 Beacon Hill Street suggested the pinnacle of Brahmin economic and social status in New England. At the age of three, however, she suffered a crippling accident while skating and was rendered immobile for most of her early childhood. Eventually she was able to walk with crutches and even to ride horses which she loved. Her other passions were reading and sailing. As to the first, the family lived next to the Boston Athenæum with its encyclopedic library, and she took full advantage, learning languages, geography, and history, which especially fascinated her. As to the second passion, sailing was a love which her indulgent father encouraged and provided opportunities for her to practice until she became quite adept in managing both small- and medium-sized craft as well as learning about charts, tides and the intricacies of managing the helm even in storms. It was a skill which would come in handy in later life.

Besides being wealthy, the family was also well connected. Dr. Osgood was a direct descendant of John Quincy Adams, for example, and had worked with Louis Pasteur who had been instrumental in bringing the first rabies antidote to the US. Molly's mother was a Cushing, a family which could trace its origins to the *Mayflower*, and although only moderately wealthy they would be connected by brilliant marriages to the Astors and the Roosevelts and other families of wealth and influence. They would have homes in New York, Boston, Newport, RI, as well as estates abroad.

In 1903 at the age of 28 Molly met the English-born writer Erskine Childers, author of the best-selling *Riddle of the Sands*. He was an English officer who had fought in the Boer War and had several Irish soldiers under his command, and he admired their courage, camaraderie and loyalty. Although also born in England, his father, Robert Erskine Childers, had an Irish mother and had been raised by an uncle in County Wicklow. His mother was a Bostonian whose ancestors arrived on the *Mayflower*. He felt that Britain made several blunders in the Boer conflict which he believed could have been resolved through careful diplomacy. He blamed Anglo superiority and contempt for the Boers for the bloodshed which followed. Although he would later go on to fight in the Great War as a British officer and be decorated for bravery, he had begun to feel a conflict of loyalties. He felt that British imperial policy was flawed and that its officers' contempt for the enlisted men was a reflection of the imperial mindset. He believed that many colonial soldiers, the Irish among them, had been needlessly sacrificed as cannon fodder by callous and often incompetent officers.

His meeting with Molly was entirely fortuitous. He was on an exchange visit between the Honorable London Artillery Company and its equivalent in Boston. He decided to remain a few days after his official duties and rented a motorcycle to explore New England. His bike broke down on the way up Beacon Hill and he stopped by the home of Dr. Childers to borrow a wrench. There he met Molly who, as a wide reader and brilliant conversationalist, struck a chord with Childers. He also had suffered an accident which left him with a gimp leg, so he sympathized with Molly's affliction. Her reading of history helped illuminate his already genuine love for Ireland, and Molly's sympathy for the growing movements for women and Irish independence were very persuasive. She introduced him to political and social luminaries in Boston society, as well as to Irish Americans who were vocal in their support for an Ireland which they hoped would be liberated from 400 years of British colonial rule. On

January 5, 1904, the couple was married in Trinity Church in Boston (the historic church in whose belfry Paul Revere set his lanterns to warn of the British invasion "One if by land two if by sea" in 1775).

The couple went to England where Childers returned to his civilian job as a Clerk of Petitions in the House of Commons. They rented a comfortable flat in Chelsea, and Childers introduced Molly to many of his friends and acquaintances, both literary and political. Like Childers, Molly admired much about England, especially its culture and literature and the part it had played in the complex tapestry of European history. But the British contempt for subject people, its institutional racism, and its exploitation of resources from smaller nations filled her with a quiet frustration. Still, they spent many pleasant hours sailing first on the *Seagull*, a boat co-owned by Childers and some university friends, then later in the *Asgard*, a 28-ton yacht Dr. Osgood gave to the young couple as a belated wedding present.

Fig. 4 Molly and Erskine Childers at the helm of the Asgard.

When British officers in Ireland opposed the Home Rule Bill and threatened to resign their commissions in support of Unionist paramilitaries, both Molly and Erskine were concerned. That worry turned to a more concerted decision to intercede when they learned that vast quantities of weapons had recently been smuggled to the Ulster Volunteers, and that former British officers were now in command of the reactionary forces. Britain's failure to either reprimand the recalcitrant officers in the first instance, or to confiscate the weapons in the second, was a clear indication that the British government was not committed to Home Rule and that Irish independence would never come about except by force. Accordingly, Erskine and Molly decided that they would put their yacht to good use, if and when the opportunity arose.

THE SHIPMENT AND HOWTH LANDING

When a deal was finally made to buy rifles from the Belgian arms dealer, the Childers offered to use the *Asgard* to transport half of the Mauser single-shot rifles and some of the crates containing the black powder ammunition. A much smaller number of Mauser rifles was to be landed from the *Chotah* at Kilcoole in County Wicklow.

Mary Spring Rice, a close friend of Molly Childers and fellow crew member of the *Asgard*, kept a diary of the journey[7] to Belgium to pick up the weapons and ammunition and transport them to Ireland. The most complete description of the voyage, the landing, and the subsequent tragedy is given in F.X. Kennedy's outstanding compendium of historical documents dating from 1914 and collected by Martin in 1964.[8] The letters and diary entries written by the chief protagonists are first-hand accounts and provide a running

---

[7]   Mary Spring Rice, "Diary of the Asgard" (https://www.anphoblacht.com/contents/24233, accessed Jan. 10, 2021).
[8]   F.X. Martin (author/editor) and Ruan O'Donnell (editor), *The Howth Gun-Running and Kilcoole Gun-Running*: Forward by Eamon de Valera (Newbridge, Kildare: Merrion, 2014).

commentary on the momentous events of July/August 1914. These rifles procured for the Irish Volunteers would transform perceptions of the organization and convince many ordinary nationalists that London would be obliged to deliver on the implementation of Home Rule. They were, of course, mistaken.

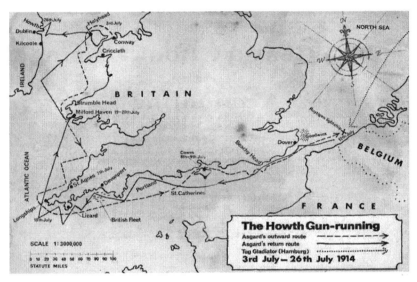

Map #1. Asgard gun-running route.

The *Asgard*, along with the *Kelpie* (owned by Childers' friend, Connor O'Brien) sailed from Milford Haven in Britain to the Ruytingen buoy near the Belgian coast. The two yachts were crewed by O'Brien, the Childers, Spring Rice, and two sailors from County Donegal. The trip over was not pleasant but this was just the beginning. As Mary Spring Rice described one day in the first leg of the journey:

Erskine, Molly and I all felt (and some of us were) extremely ill. Poor Molly had to lie down in her cabin, so was much the worst off. I felt just able to survive while I stayed on deck, and all afternoon the wind rose. It was SE and there was lots of it, and a very choppy short sea

29

into which the *Asgard* drove her bows. I curled up in an unhappy heap on the cockpit floor, cold and miserable, in a leaky oilskin...the *Asgard* now looked extremely small, a mere cockleshell on the waves, and I wondered how long it would go on like this. (Saturday, July 4, 1914).

After a week of sailing, they met up with the tugboat that had carried the rifles from Hamburg on the evening of July 11th. Mary Spring Rice describes in detail the backbreaking labor required to fit all the rifles and ammunition into the diminutive cabin space below. Leaving anything on deck could get the cargo impounded and the crew arrested if observed by any passing English warship or coast guard cutter. Anything unable to fit below would have to be left behind, a prospect none could face.

We hastily hauled bags of clothes and mattresses and stowed them aft of the mizzen. As the tug came up, Darrell Figgis called from her deck that Conor had taken 600 rifles and 20,000 rounds of ammunition. "He's left you 900 and 29,000 rounds," he shouted. We looked at each other. Could we even take them? We had only counted on 750 and they looked enormous, each thickly done up in straw.

The tug looked black and huge alongside us. Her deck was full of German sailors who jabbered away and looked curiously at us as they passed down the big canvas bales.

I found myself in the saloon...passing down rifles through the skylight, and we packing them in, butts at the end and barrels in the centre, as fast as we could. They came in bales of ten and we counted them as we stowed them: "8, 9, 10; steady a minute, Pat, till I stow this one." Inside the cabin, Erskine and Molly were doing the same thing. 40 went into the port bunk in the saloon. Should we ever get them all in?

It was fearfully hot work. They were fairly heavy and thick with grease, which made them horrible to handle. Gradually, however, the pile grew and presently the saloon was half full, level with the table, and we went up on deck to help strip straw off as they could hardly hand them down fast enough. Then when we had undone a certain number below again to pack them in.

So it went on through the night. Still, bale after bale of rifles were passed down from the tug, and every now and again we shouted to the German crew to know how many more were still to come. And the saloon got full, and the cabin and the passage, and then we began to put on another layer, and to pile them at the foot of the companion hatch.

Meanwhile, the ammunition had been coming down in fearfully heavy boxes, which were stowed with infinite labour aft under the cockpit, a very difficult place to get at, at the foot of the companion, in the sail lockers, and a couple in the fo'castle. Erskine was very keen to take all the ammunition we possibly could and certainly it seemed rather a sin to leave it to be put overboard by the tug, and aboard it all came somehow. Several boxes were left on the deck till we could make room to stow them. Personally, I felt rather nervous as to the effect this tremendous extra weight would have on the yacht in bad weather, but Erskine's one thought was to take everything. (Sunday, July 12, 1914).

There was no room to prepare food and no time, so Molly broke out chocolate bars and literally broke pieces off and put them in people's mouths as they labored to get the rifles and heavy crates of ammunition aboard. They worked away throughout the night until, as the faint light of dawn appeared on the horizon, all the crates and rifles were safely stowed below. There was no room to lie down or to cook meals. It was to be an uncomfortable journey to Ireland. They could only hope and pray for good weather and that they would not be intercepted by a British destroyer.

On the return journey, they first met with bad storms. Next, they encountered an entire fleet of the Royal Navy out on maneuvers in anticipation of the outbreak of war. They could not go around without incurring suspicion so had to sail through the fleet with their illicit cargo. If any of the British officers decided to give an order to board, the German guns would be confiscated, and they would all face many years in an English prison. In 19 days, August 4, 1914, Great Britain would formally declare war against Germany. Caught transporting German weapons at that time, they could all face death for treason. Quickly, both Molly and Mary grabbed large

Fig. 5. Molly Childers and Mary Spring Rice on the last leg of the journey.

cushions and covered up the crates on the deck. One destroyer passed close to the *Asgard.*

> I stood holding up the stern light on the starboard side, watching her getting nearer and nearer, with my heart in my mouth. Then, mercifully, at the last moment she changed her course and passed us by. (Thursday, July 16, 1914).

Five days later they were stopped by a British coast guard cutter which did not board them but shouted questions over to Erskine Childers who was at the helm. *Last port? Registered tonnage? Owner's name?* He responded, confidently mixing fiction with fact, and they were allowed to go on. That time, someone had the presence of mind to throw a sail over the crates that were on the dock, and nothing appeared amiss. It was fortunate since the cutter came up quickly and without warning.

On the evening of Friday, July 24 the seas were rough with howling winds and towering waves. The crew suffered with wet clothes, bitter cold, and no sleep. The danger of losing sail, or even capsizing with a full load was real. Mary recalled, "The waves looked black and terrible and enormous, and though everything was reefed one wondered if we should get through without something giving way."

At last, on Sunday, July 26 at one o'clock in the afternoon they arrived safely at Howth Harbor. A long line of armed Volunteers marched down the hill to greet them, as well as members of Fianna Éireann with hand carts and wheelbarrows led by Countess Markiewicz. Then, suddenly, a coast guard boat from across the harbor appeared approaching rapidly. The volunteers drew their revolvers on them. Rather than engage in a one-sided battle, the captain elected to fire off rocket signals for help.

A fleet of taxis arrived, and the Volunteers and the young men were able to offload all the rifles. After appropriating some of the weapons for themselves, they put the remainder and the crates of ammunition into taxis and spirited them away. It happened so swiftly that the *Asgard* and her crew were able to escape before more British boats could arrive. Meanwhile, the harbor master informed the authorities of the violation, and the Dublin Metropolitan Police were called out as well as a detachment of troops from the Kilmainham barracks. The two groups would meet at the village of Clontarf.

There was a clear desire on the part of the Volunteers to confront authority at this point. They wanted to let the British know that if they wished to turn a blind eye to the Unionists arming themselves, they must give way to the Nationalists as well. But there was another more important, symbolic reason they wished for a confrontation. As they headed to the Dublin City Centre, the newly armed Volunteers were met by a detachment of British soldiers on one side and police on the other at the southern tip of Clontarf. Now Clontarf, as every Irish child who listened to grandfather's stories by the peat fire knew, was an important part of Irish history. It was the location of the famous battle in which BrianBorú, the great King of Ireland, defeated the Norse and freed Ireland from foreign oppression in 1014. Now, 900 years later, his descendants were called upon again. A struggle ensued between Volunteers and the police. Many policemen refused to obey orders to disarm the Volunteers and those that followed orders were unable to seize the weapons. As they moved forward, they faced another confrontation with the military detachment in which there was more hand-to-hand fighting involving bayonets and rifle butts. But the army backed down as well and the Volunteers moved on victoriously, singing patriotic songs as they marched to Dublin city center.

THE BACHELOR'S WALK MASSACRE

As the disheartened soldiers headed back to their barracks, crowds began to gather alongside the road leading to Kilmainham and they began to taunt the soldiers and accuse them of cowardice. The jeers continued as they reached Bachelor's Walk and an officer who joined them en route stopped the column and gave the order to raise their weapons and confront the crowd. While he was addressing the civilians, a shot was fired by one of the troops and this was followed by a volley. Three people were killed instantly. Then followed a bayonet charge on the crowd to force them back. Thirty more were seriously injured and one died later from bayonet wounds. Pádraic Pearse declared: "The army is an object of odium, and the Volunteers are the heroes of the hour. The whole movement, the whole country, has been re-baptised (sic) by bloodshed for Ireland."[9] Nine days later, Britain would declare war on Germany. But waiting in the wings was an Irish revolution that was slowly circling in its winding gyre.

A year later, Pearse would remind his listeners again of the heroic dead in the Glasnevin Cemetery as he gave the funeral oration for O'Donovan Rossa, a loyal Fenian and a prominent member of the Irish Republican Brotherhood. His carefully chosen words, penned in the quiet solitude of his Connemara cottage, would echo for generations to come.

The Defenders of the Realm have worked well in secret and in the open. They think they have pacified Ireland. They think they have purchased half of us and intimidated the other half. They think they have foreseen everything, think they have provided against everything; but the fools, the fools, the fools! —they have left us our Fenian dead, and while Ireland holds these graves, Ireland unfree shall never be at peace.

---

[9]   Turtle Bunbury, "Death on Bachelor's Walk –26 July 1914" on TurtleBunbury.com (https://www.turtlebunbury.com/history/history_irish/history_irish_bachelors_ walk.htm, accessed Jan. 12, 2021).

4

ALICE STOPFORD GREEN
AND SIR ROGER CASEMENT

G reen was not only instrumental in supplying ready cash for
the Howth rifles, but she was also a major influence in wider
circles. As a highly respected historian, she was in constant contact
with intellectuals both in the British Isles and on the Continent,
as well as with diplomats and officials. Her home in Kensington
Square became a meeting place for such luminaries as the writer
Henry James and the justice Oliver Wendell Holmes, as well as
French diplomats and Irish artists including the well-known painter
Jack Yeats and the author and Fenian John O'Leary who was im-
mortalized in William Butler Yeats' poem.[10] Since her 1908 book,
The Making of Ireland and Its Undoing, she had written two more:
Irish Nationality (1911) and *The Old Irish World* (1912) which showed
what Ireland had been before the British conquest and what it could
be again when no longer subservient to Britain. A free Ireland at
peace, culturally and economically connected to Europe and the
wider world, no longer economically dependent on the whims of
the Crown, she suggested, was within reach.[11]

Her friendship with Casement went back many years and they
had come together once on the shipment of arms for the Volunteers.
But that work was unfinished. With more than 15,000 Volunteers
and Irish Citizen Army recruits, the 1,500 rifles landed at Howth

[10] As William Butler Yeats wrote in "September 1913": "Romantic Ireland's dead and
gone; it's with O'Leary in the grave.".

[11] This was a prescient vision and one which has relevance today. With the
departure of the UK from the European Union after Brexit, a referendum on an
independent Scotland in the offing, a united Ireland as part of the wider Eurozone
is not only possible but, many believe, highly likely.

would not be nearly enough. She encouraged Casement to keep working on this problem, not only raising money but using his diplomatic contacts to buy more guns.

Like Erskine Childers, she was upset by the brutal policies of the British in South Africa and the atrocities of the Boer War. She was also a vocal supporter of the Congo Reform Movement initiated by Casement when he was in the British service in Africa. She was a proponent of Home Rule and, when it became apparent that the movement would be shelved or met with violence by Unionists, she wanted to find ways to move forward. When Casement asked her to help with a loan to purchase weapons, she did not hesitate. Having access to funds both from her husband's legacy and her own writing, she supplied the group with a significant loan to begin negotiations with arms dealers.

SIR ROGER CASEMENT

Considered the father of twentieth-century human rights investigations, the Dublin-born diplomat Roger Casement was honored both for his exposé of conditions in the Congo and for documenting human rights violations in Peru. In 1911 he was knighted by King George V for his service to humanity.

Casement had worked in the Congo for Henry Morton Stanley and the African International Association. Later he was asked to conduct an official investigation of conditions there on behalf of the British government. In the performance of his duties, he uncovered the atrocities of King Leopold II of Belgium who had been using the African country as his own private reserve for extracting minerals, diamonds, and ivory, as well as the harvesting of rubber on a massive scale. Leopold had essentially enslaved the population and taken over vast tracts of acreage to produce rubber, a scarce commodity before the invention of a synthetic substitute. Enriching himself enormously, he used whippings and horrific mutilations (such as cutting off the hands of those who did not meet their quotas) in the pursuit of his global business. He ordered tens of thousands of elephants killed for their ivory. He enslaved hundreds of villages for the harvesting of rubber, garnering a 700 percent profit in rubber sales which went directly into his coffers since he literally had no labor costs or overhead. Joseph Conrad, author of *The Heart of Darkness,* called his practices "the vilest scramble for loot that ever disfigured the history of human conscience."[12] Instead of durable goods for the natives, he shipped guns, whips and machetes to the overseers and his 19,000-man army, called *Force Publique*, to keep the people in line. Casement traveled throughout the region and produced a stunning eyewitness account of the horrors. As a result of his report, the Belgian parliament removed the Congo from Leopold's control.[13]

Influenced by his observations of imperial control and abuse of smaller nations, Casement retired from the consular service due to poor health in 1913 with a strong distrust of colonialism and a determination to do something about it. His meetings with Alice Stopford Green helped him to envision an Ireland which treasured its rich past and traditions and could become once again a great nation united in its self-determination. Upon his return to Ireland, he joined Arthur Griffith's new Sinn Fein party which proposed an independent Ireland. He joined other like-minded Irish expats in the Gaelic League to support the revitalization of Irish language and literature.

In November of 1913 he helped organize the Irish Volunteers. Along with Eoin MacNeill he co-wrote the Volunteers' manifesto. After several meetings with Alice Stopford Green, Molly and Erskine Childers, Michael O'Rahilly and others to raise money for arms, he traveled to America on a fundraising mission, and spoke to many Irish American communities on the East Coast. There, he

[12] Joseph Conrad, *Last Essays* (edited by Harold Ray Stephens. London: Cambridge University Press, 2010, Kindle Edition).
[13] One of the best books on the subject is *King Leopold's Ghost: A Story of Greed, Terror and Heroism in Colonial Africa* by Adam Hochschild (New York: Mariner Books, 1999).

also established contact with the exiled Irish nationalists in the Clan na Gael.

In the fall of 1914, he travelled to Germany (via Norway) in disguise to recruit an Irish brigade among the 2,000 Irish prisoners-of-war captured by the Germans and held in a POW camp. They were part of a large group of Allied soldiers captured during the retreat from Mons and the battles which followed in August and September of 1914. However, Casement had only limited success in this endeavor. Only 52 of the prisoners volunteered. In April 1916, Casement negotiated with the German government to purchase 20,000 Mosin-Nagant 1892 rifles, ten machine guns, several crates of high explosives and fuses, and a million rounds of ammunition. Plans were then made to transport the cargo to Ireland. This was only a week before the Rising.

A German cargo ship disguised as a Norwegian transport vessel with the name *Aud-Norge* on its bow was loaded with the weapons along with a German crew disguised as Norwegian sailors. Casement went ahead in a German submarine which put him ashore at Banna Strand off Tralee Bay, County Kerry in the early hours of April 21.

THE ROYAL NAVY INTERCEPT OF THE *AUD-NORGE*

The *Aud-Norge* left Germany on April 9 with a crew of 22 sailors and German navy captain Karl Spindler headed for Tralee Bay as well. It was not expected to arrive until Sunday 23. The ship did not have radio telegraph communication so when it arrived in Tralee Bay early, on April 21 there was no answering signal from the shore. Meanwhile the British had intercepted communications coming from Washington that indicated there might be a shipment of arms attempting to land in Ireland. Although they had no information about the exact location, they put the entire fleet in the area on high alert.

When Captain Spindler received no answering signals from the beach, he proceeded to cruise to an offshore island and wait for darkness to leave the bay. Suddenly, he was spotted by a British cruiser, the HMS *Bluebell*. He headed for the open sea but was soon cut off by British warships and given the order to follow them to Cork Harbor, Queenstown.

During the night as they headed for Cork Harbor, Captain Spindler ordered the crew to plant explosive charges throughout the ship. As they entered the harbor, he evacuated his crew in lifeboats. Then he raised the German ensign and abandoned the ship himself as his first mate detonated the charges. Within minutes the ship was scuttled and sank bow-up into the sea. Spindler and his crew were captured and taken to a POW camp in England.

Meanwhile, Roger Casement, stricken with recurrent malarial fever that he had contracted in the Congo, was too weak to travel. He was discovered by a sergeant in the Royal Constabulary at McKenna's Fort (an ancient ring fortification now called Casement's Fort) and arrested. He was charged with high treason, sabotage, and espionage against the Crown, all of which carried the death penalty. His was the first sacrifice of the Rising because, while there were sufficient volunteers in the Kerry Brigade to overcome the Constabulary and rescue him and they were quite willing to do so, they had been ordered by the Dublin leadership to stand down and do nothing. Not a gun should be fired until the actual Rising lest they tip their hand too early. Roger Casement would be hanged in London on August 3, 1916, and buried naked in a common grave with a notorious murderer hanged earlier. It was a final gesture of contempt by the British overlords who saw his love for his own country as a betrayal of theirs. He was the first of the Irish rebels to be captured and the last to die.

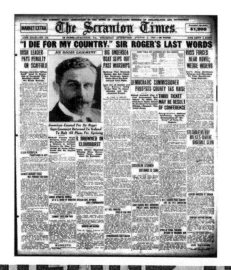

Fig. 6. *Scranton Times* and *Atlanta Constitution*, August 3, 1916.

5

CONSTANCE MARKIEWICZ AND THE BOYS OF FIANNA ÉIREANN

Constance Markiewicz was a stately dark-haired beauty, who led her group of teenage boys up the hills and across the valleys near her estate. Borrowing from the Boy Scouts, she coached her troops in personal hygiene, first aid, and civic responsibility. She also trained them in military maneuvers and taught them to fire rifles and pistols. At six foot one she was an imposing figure and her knowledge of weaponry and tactics impressed not only the boys, but even the local men who knew her. To top it all off, she was a noblewoman, with a large estate and some personal wealth, as well as a position in the Ascendancy, or Anglo-Irish upper class. She harbored radical ideas, however, about the legitimacy of the ruling class, and the plight of Irish workers. Even more dangerous for the authorities, she had developed a commitment to the removal of English rule and the independence of Ireland.

Born Constance Georgina Gore-Booth in London in 1868, she was the daughter of the Arctic explorer Sir Henry Gore-Booth and his wife Georgina. Her father was also an Anglo-Irish landlord who was considered quite liberal and even provided free food to his tenants at their estate in County Sligo during the second Irish Famine of 1879-80. Her father's example was to motivate both Constance and her younger sister Eva with a concern for the poor and for working people. The two sisters were also childhood friends of William Butler Yeats, who visited their estate in Sligo and inspired them with his love for ancient Irish folk tales and lore. He also encouraged both sisters to write their own verse. Eva would become part of the Celtic revival that swept over Ireland at the turn of the twentieth century, and was the author of nine books of poetry, seven plays, and several collections of spiritual essays and pamphlets in support of women's rights. Constance, on the other hand, was better known for her rousing pamphlets in support of the labor movement and Irish independence. She also authored several patriotic songs. Eva was a pacifist, while Constance, as we shall see, was nothing of the kind.

In her twenties, Constance went to study art in London at the Slade School of Art, the only art academy that accepted women. There she became politically involved with the women's suffrage movement. After a course of studies, she moved to Paris where she met Casimir Markiewicz, a Polish nobleman. He and Constance fell in love and married and she thus became Countess Markiewicz, by which name she has been known throughout history.

Shortly after their marriage the couple moved to Ireland where Constance became involved with James Connolly's Irish Citizen Army which was a socialist militia formed to defend demonstrating workers from the police. Police brutality, even murder of strikers, was not only ignored by the British but passively encouraged by the laissez-faire policy of the governing body towards industrialists and factory owners, who had the active protection of local police and instructions to put down any lockdown or strike with force.

During the Transport Workers' strike in 1913, Constance opened her house as a place of refuge where strikers could find both a place to sleep and meals. In addition, she sold some of her jewels to establish soup kitchens for their families. About this time Baden Powell was organizing the British Boy Scouts in Ireland and was very impressed with the work that Pádraig Pearse was doing with Irish boys. Pearse had opened a school at his own expense to teach boys Irish language and history and well as the traditional subjects. His belief was that Irish culture was being steadily eroded by the British occupation and would eventually disappear if something was not done.

Fig. 7. Constance Markiewicz and her cocker spaniel, Poppet.

When Powell suggested he should help him form a Boy Scout troop, Pearse demurred. He was an Irish nationalist and had no intention of training boys to become potential British soldiers However, he passed the word to Constance, and she took up the banner but with a twist. She would train them to become Irish freedom fighters. Working with Bulmer Hobson, an early scout organizer, she named the group Fianna Éireann, after a military organization during the reign of Cormac MacAirt, one of the ancient Irish heroes. By 1914 the Markiewicz home on Leinster Road became headquarters for the group. According to one who knew her well, she was loved and trusted by the boys she trained.

The house in Leinster Road was always running over with the lads, some as young as ten years. You would find them studying hard, or just as likely, sliding down fine old banisters. Madam never went anywhere that they did not follow as bodyguards. They loved her and trusted her, a high compliment, since I have always found that boys are keen judges of sincerity. [14]

Fig. 8. Constance Markiewicz in 1916.

[14] Margaret Skinnider, *Doing My Bit for Ireland* (London: Kindle edition, 2016), loc 164-167.

She was a trained marksman used to hunting and was able to impart those skills to the boys who trained under her. As a member of the Ascendancy, she was allowed to import weapons into the country and had shotguns, Enfield rifles, Mauser machine pistols, and even Colts at her home. When the boys turned 17, most joined the Irish Citizen Army, Sinn Fein,[15] or the Irish Volunteers. Some who were even younger when the actual fighting broke out joined as well.

For now, she was content to train the boys, write patriotic songs, design the dark green uniforms for the Citizen Army, and write dozens of pamphlets in support of Irish autonomy and against conscription of Irish lads to fight in the British Army. In August of 1916, Great Britain declared war against Germany and began mustering millions of men from their colonies to support their war effort. The countess and her friends and allies had a different vision.

---

[15] The Sinn Fein ("We Ourselves", pronounced "Shin Fayn") was originally a small nationalist/sociality party. However, when the Irish Volunteers in 1914 split on the issue of support for the British Army in World War I, many Volunteers enlisted. Those who remained behind to fight for the republic were sometimes known as Sinn Fein Volunteers. The British made much of this and called the Rising "the Sinn Fein Rebellion" in many reports and newspaper articles. Thus, the party grew in popularity and membership increased to many thousands after the Rising.

6

EARLY CONFUSION, BOLD BEGINNING

The official stance of the Irish Volunteers was that action would only be taken if the British authorities at Dublin Castle attempted to disarm the Volunteers or introduce conscription to Ireland to get more young men into their army. Some members of the Irish Republican Brotherhood (IRB),[16] however, were determined to use the Volunteers for offensive action while Britain was tied up in World War I.

Although the Rising was originally planned for Easter Sunday, an order was issued countermanding that decision and informing all volunteers to stand down. This order was issued by Eoin MacNeill on Good Friday to members of Irish Volunteers in all the counties of Ireland, after he had been informed that the expected shipment of arms from Germany would not be forthcoming. He believed that without those arms, military action at this time would result in defeat and great loss of life.

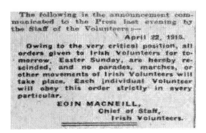

Fig. 9. Eoin MacNeill's order of April 22, 1916.

---

[16]   The Irish Republican Brotherhood (IRB) was the secret organization founded in 1858 and dedicated to attaining national independence and national sovereignty for a 32-county Ireland. Its members planned the Easter Rising and composed most of the leadership.

In Dublin, however, other leaders regarded this decision as pusillanimous and also felt that to stand down now would be an irreversible setback. Military strategist Thomas Clarke, socialist leader James Connolly, and commander Pádraic Pearse met in council and decided to go ahead with the Rising on the day after Easter, April 24. This decision, however, was not communicated to the outlying counties due to the limitations of technology and the need for secrecy. Thus, as the day approached, most of the rebels around the country were still at home unaware as 1250 members of the Irish Volunteers and 219 soldiers of the Irish Citizen Army (ICA) were assembling in the capital.[17]

Although the ICA was the only group that accepted women recruits as armed combatants in their ranks, over 300 women were an integral part of the Rising. The Irish Volunteer Army also employed women as messengers, gun-runners, transport workers, and medical staff where they were exposed to enemy fire. Officially they were known as the Cumann na mBan, or Women's Council.

On 23 April 1916, when the Military Council of the Irish Republican Brotherhood finalized arrangements for the Rising, it integrated Cumann na mBan, along with the Irish Volunteers and the Irish Citizen Army, into the "Army of the Irish Republic" or, as it became better known, the Irish Republican Army (IRA). Pádraic Pearse was appointed Commandant-General and James Connolly Commandant-General of the Dublin Division. [18]

---

[17] There were also actions by the Volunteers outside of Dublin. A small contingent attacked the Royal Irish Constabulary in County Meath, there were also actions in County Wexford, County Cork, as well as County Laois, County Lowth and County Galway. Those involved in these skirmishes numbered about a thousand. See John Dorney, " The Easter Rising in County Wexford," (*The Irish Story*, 10 April 2012) and "The Easter Rising in County Galway 1916," (*The Irish Story*, 4 March 2016).

[18] Lil Conlon, "Cumann na mBan and the Women of Ireland 1913–1925." (Kilkenny: *Kilkenny People (1916), 33. https://kec1916project.files.wordpress.com/2015/02/the-kilkenny-people-reports-the-rising.pdf*, accessed Jan. 10, 2021.)

EASTER - APRIL 23, 1916

James Connolly's eldest daughter, Nora, returned with six members of her female contingent from the north, where she had gone to help with the mobilization of the Volunteers in County Tyrone. Nora had been involved in politics with her father from a very early age. She was one of the founders of the Young Republican Army and the girls' branch of the Fianna, the Irish scouts. She was a founding member of the Cumann na mBan in the north. She helped carry ammunition and rifles for Erskine Childers after the 1914 Howth landing, after which she and her sister were rewarded with two rifles from the shipment.

She was shocked when news arrived that the Northern Division of the Irish Volunteers was being demobilized because of a message from Eoin MacNeill to the effect that the Easter Uprising had been cancelled because the shipment of arms had been intercepted. Nora was incredulous and hurried back to Dublin to inform her father. When she arrived at Liberty Hall at 6am, her father had just gone to bed after a night of planning. She had the sentry wake him up with the news that the Volunteers from the north would not be coming. He was visibly upset and had tears in his eyes. When Nora asked him if it was true that they were not going to fight, he replied, "If we don't fight now, the only thing we can do is pray for an earthquake to come and swallow us up, and our shame."[19] He asked her and her contingent to get the leadership together and have them come to Liberty Hall for a meeting. Seán MacDermott, Thomas MacDonagh, Joseph Plunkett, Éamonn Ceannt and Pádraic Pearse quickly arrived. Nora served them breakfast and afterwards attended a meeting during which it was determined that the Uprising would still continue but at noon the next day, Easter Monday. Connolly ordered leaders to send out word to the rest of the Dublin Volunteers and Citizen Army members.

---

[19] Statement by Mrs. Nora Connolly O'Brien, Bureau of Military History (https://www.militaryarchives.ie/collections/online-collections/bureau-of-military-history-1913-1921/reels/bmh/BMH.WS0286.pdf, accessed Jan. 10, 2021.)

Connolly was in a much better mood once he had made his decision. Nora remembered that he was going around the room singing "We have got another savior now/That savior is the sword."[20] The die had been cast. Meanwhile men had gathered around Liberty Hall as word got out to the Volunteers. The Citizen Army already knew that they were going to fight. Now the Dublin Volunteers would learn it as well. Conolly was effectively countermanding MacNeill's demobilization order. At around 4pm he gathered all the men and gave them a brief talk. Nora Connolly faithfully recorded it.

> We have been playing at soldiers for a long time, but the time has come to be soldiers in real earnest. If there is anyone, who, for any reason, mystic or otherwise, is not prepared to go the whole way with us, let him step out now. There will be no hard words or hard feelings. It would be better for him to do so now, than to come along with us and let us rely upon him, and then to fail us when he was most needed.[21]

No one stepped out even after he walked up and down the whole ranks of men and repeated, "Let him step out now. There will be no hard words or hard feelings."

Then with his hands clasped behind his back and his eyes shining, he said, "Boys, I never doubted you!"[22]

He dismissed them with orders that they were to return no later than 10 o' clock the following morning. Nora spent the night at Constance Markiewicz's home on Leinster Road, and then returned to Liberty Hall the following morning.

[20] Ibid., 34
[21] Ibid., 37.
[22] Ibid.

Fig. 10. Nora Conolly in her Irish Volunteers' uniform.

EASTER MONDAY – APRIL 24, 2016

There were heavy rains the night before and the morning was overcast and chilly, about 40F°. The clouds hung low and there was a brisk breeze. The four battalions of the Army of the Irish Republic were assembled and given orders to proceed to various points in Dublin center.

Shortly after 11:00 the combined forces began to move to strategic locations within the city to capture buildings and set up blockades. Commandant Michael Mallin of the Irish Citizen Army joined by Countess Markiewicz and 100 men and women began digging trenches in St. Stephen's Green just south of Grafton Street and commandeering passing vehicles in order to make barriers on the surrounding streets. Other rebels took buildings around the park including the Royal College of Surgeons.

The Dublin branch of the Irish Volunteers were divided into four battalions. The first battalion under Ned Daly was made up of about 250 men and it would occupy the Four Courts building, apart from D Company, led by Seán Heuston, whose 26 men would occupy the Mendicity Institution, across the Liffey River from the Four Courts.

The second battalion, led by Commandant Thomas MacDonagh, assembled at St. Stephen's Green but were ordered to move out and take Jacob's Biscuit Factory, another key position.

The third battalion was commanded by American-born Eamon de Valera, and it would take Boland's Mills. Reserved and introspective, de Valera was respected by his men because of his courage and his ability to think clearly and strategize under pressure.

The fourth battalion, led by Éamonn Ceannt and numbering about 100 men, moved in on the South Dublin Union (SDU) near the rail line from the southwest in order to intercept British troops coming from the base in County Kildare. It was here that a nurse, by the name of Margaret Keogh, would be shot by a British soldier as she came to the aid of the wounded.

Noon: Although not without incident, the General Post Office (GPO) on Sackville Street (now O'Connell Street) was stormed by the rebels. Customers and staff were ordered to leave the building. Those who showed defiance were prodded with rifle butts. In addition, several British soldiers present were taken prisoner and the windows were smashed so the spaces could be reinforced by furniture and other barriers to be used as a defensive shield against attack from without. Those who were not in the first four battalions, as well as several leaders, would now be in this building, which would also be general headquarters for the remainder of the insurrection. They included Pádraic Pearse, Tom Clarke, Joseph Plunkett and Séan MacDermott.

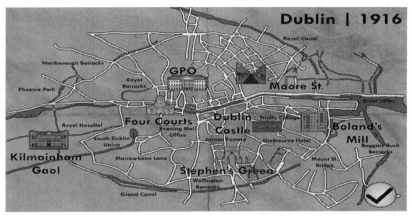

Map #2. Central Dublin in 1916.

12:30: The green, white and orange tricolor was raised above the GPO, along with a green flag bearing the words "Irish Republic", and the rebels completed the boarding-up of the front of the building as well as blockading key points along Sackville Street.[23] They were met with no resistance. A number of civilians had gathered along the street to see what was happening. Most were confused and had no idea that a revolt was actually taking place.

12:45: Commander-in-Chief Pádraic Pearse emerged from the GPO to read aloud the Proclamation which he had written to declare the independent Irish Republic.

---

[23]   This was not the first Irish flag raised in Dublin. Another was one hoisted by James Connolly's company at City Hall. The very first defiant flag, however, was that raised by a 16-year-old girl named Mary ("Molly") O'Reilly. On Palm Sunday, eight days before the Rising, Molly raised the green flag with the gold harp over Liberty Hall.

POBLACHT NA hÉIREANN
THE PROVISIONAL GOVERNMENT
OF THE
IRISH REPUBLIC
TO THE PEOPLE OF IRELAND

IRISHMEN AND IRISHWOMEN: In the name of God and of the dead generations from which she receives her old tradition of nationhood, Ireland, through us, summons her children to her flag and strikes for her freedom.

Having organised and trained her manhood through her secret revolutionary organisation, the Irish Republican Brotherhood, and through her open military organisations, the Irish Volunteers and the Irish Citizen Army, having patiently perfected her discipline, having resolutely waited for the right moment to reveal itself, she now seizes that moment, and supported by her exiled children in America and by gallant allies in Europe, but relying in the first on her own strength, she strikes in full confidence of victory.

We declare the right of the people of Ireland to the ownership of Ireland and to the unfettered control of Irish destinies, to be sovereign and indefeasible. The long usurpation of that right by a foreign people and government has not extinguished the right, nor can it ever be extinguished except by the destruction of the Irish people. In every generation the Irish people have asserted their right to national freedom and sovereignty; six times during the past three hundred years they have asserted it in arms. Standing on that fundamental right and again asserting it in arms in the face of the world, we hereby proclaim the Irish Republic as a Sovereign Independent State, and we pledge our lives and the lives of our comrades in arms to the cause of its freedom, of its welfare, and of its exaltation among the nations.

The Irish Republic is entitled to, and hereby claims, the allegiance of every Irishman and Irishwoman. The Republic guarantees religious and civil liberty, equal rights and equal opportunities to all its citizens, and declares its resolve to pursue the happiness and prosperity of the whole nation and of all its parts, cherishing all of the children of the nation equally, and oblivious of the differences carefully fostered by an alien Government, which have divided a minority from the majority in the past.

Until our arms have brought the opportune moment for the establishment of a permanent National Government, representative of the whole people of Ireland and elected by the suffrages of all her men and women, the Provisional Government, hereby constituted, will administer the civil and military affairs of the Republic in trust for the people.

We place the cause of the Irish Republic under the protection of the Most High God, Whose blessing we invoke upon our arms, and we pray that no one who serves that cause will dishonour it by cowardice, inhumanity, or rapine. In this supreme hour the Irish nation must, by its valour and discipline, and by the readiness of its children to sacrifice themselves for the common good, prove itself worthy of the august destiny to which it is called.

Signed on behalf of the Provisional Government:

THOMAS J. CLARKE
SEAN Mac DIARMADA THOMAS MacDONAGH
P. H. PEARSE EAMONN CEANNT
JAMES CONNOLLY JOSEPH PLUNKETT

Pearse believed that he would accomplish several things by the proclamation. First, he would announce to the world that this was a legitimate armed uprising by an organized militia. This was especially important to relay to the US with several million Irish Americans who were sympathetic and two citizens who were actually leaders of the Rising. Second, that as a recognized and uniformed army, no matter what the outcome, the combatants should all be treated as prisoners of war if captured. Third, by announcing to the Irish citizens the substance of the cause, he would enlist their broad support.

The seven signatories, members of the provisional government, declared the right of the people of Ireland to the ownership of Ireland but they also guaranteed religious and civil liberty, equal rights, and equal opportunities to all its citizens. And finally, to ensure the legitimacy of the enterprise, by invoking the Rules of War they declared their firm commitment to avoid rapine, killing of civilians, or mistreatment of prisoners.

The document was printed in secret several days before it was distributed amongst the public. Now, as it was being read aloud by Pearse, it was ignored by most of the crowd, although some in attendance applauded it as a work of inspiration, establishing as it did all citizens of Ireland on equal footing – men, women, and children. It was also approved for praising the work of Irish emigrants on behalf of the Irish cause, in particular "her exiled children in America" without whose support the Rising might never have happened.

To the average Dublin citizen, the storming of the GPO and other buildings by the rebels on this damp and chilly morning was not a cause for celebration. Most were frustrated as they attempted to carry on with their normal lives. They were unhappy with the unrest and violence brought to their streets. Others were outraged by the confiscation of their vehicles or their office furniture to be used as barricades on Sackville Street and the streets bordering St. Stephen's Green.

7
ROSIE HACKETT, A DUBLIN WORKER

An important link to the Proclamation, Rosie Hackett was instrumental in the printing and distribution of the final document. Born into a working-class Dublin family, Rosie Hackett co-founded the Irish Women Workers Union to combat the deplorable conditions endured by the female employees of Jacob's Biscuit Factory.

Fig. 11. Memorial plaque for Rosie Hackett, after whom a Dublin bridge and also a hospital are named. No photos exist of her as a young woman in the Rising.

Hackett's first job was with Jacob's Biscuit Factory where she worked as a packer in 1911. Still in her teens, she was appalled by the working conditions in the factory and helped organize the women in the factory to support the striking men. While the union obtained some reforms, management resisted any substantial changes.

At the age of eighteen she co-founded the Irish Women's Working Union and two years later the men and women workers combined and staged a lockout to obtain a raise in wages and healthier working conditions. She also set up soup kitchens for the striking workers. A year later she was fired by the company for her organizational activities.

Unfazed, she got a new job as a clerk at a printing establishment in Liberty Hall and became involved with James Connolly's Irish Citizen Army which was preparing for the inevitable revolt against Britain. She assisted the printers with broadsides, Pádraig Pearse's pamphlets, the rebel newspaper *The Gael,* and eventually the Proclamation.

Six months before the Rising, she began training as a medic under the supervision of Dr. Kathleen Lynn. She also participated in night marches and simulated raids with the ICA. Dr. Lynn was the Chief Medical Officer of the Irish Republican Army, and she also used her car to secretly transport weapons to the troops. She kept a detailed account of her activities in a journal which is how we know so much about the women involved. Hackett also participated in some of this clandestine work, carrying messages and guns to the Republican Army under the wary eyes of British soldiers and Dublin constables.

By their own admission it was sometimes risky work and could have resulted in imprisonment. On one occasion the print shop where she was working was raided by the Royal Irish Constabulary looking for copies of the underground newspaper *The Gael.* Alone in the shop, Hackett pretended that there were other staff and told the police to please wait. She went downstairs and contacted James Connolly and his assistant Helena Molony, both of whom were armed. While they held off the police, Hackett removed all the copies of the paper to a safe place. When the police later returned with armed reinforcements, they were unable to find anything incriminating.

It is important to remember that small amounts of weapons for personal defense were tolerated by the British since they knew that the Unionists were spoiling for trouble over the Home Rule business, and they considered that the Irish Free Staters had a right to defend themselves. It was this anomaly of 1916 which gave the rebels a strong sense that the time had indeed come for the Rising.

At any rate, neither she nor Pearse were to linger outside the GPO on this early afternoon of Easter Monday, April 24 as the 6th Cavalry unit, the first of the British regiments to arrive on the scene, moved in and cleared the streets, forcing the crowds to disperse.

8

MARGARET KEOGH AND
THE FIRST FATALITIES

Within the first two hours of Easter Monday rebels had stormed and occupied several of the capital city's most important political and economic buildings: Jacob's Factory, the Four Courts, St. Stephen's Green, the South Dublin Union, Jameson Distillery, the Mendicity Institute, Boland's Mills and Bakery and the GPO, plus 25 Northumberland Road and Clanwilliam House. They attempted to seize weapons from the Magazine Fort in Phoenix Park but, despite disarming the guards, they failed to obtain any arms.

The first official fatality of the rebellion was a non-combatant, by the name of Margaret Keogh, a nurse attempting to tend to the injured.

Her death occurred during the battle for the South Dublin Union (SDU). As she attempted to save a wounded citizen-soldier, Dan McCarthy, she was shot by a British soldier at the doorway of the Acute Hospital or Hospital 3. She was the first person to die in the insurrection, succumbing from her wounds in the early afternoon of Monday April 24. She was in a nurse's uniform at the time, and it was apparent she was a non-combatant. The British soldier who shot her was never prosecuted or reprimanded.

Nurse Keogh was born and raised in Orchard, Leighlinbridge, County Carlow, and was the niece of Captain Myles Keogh of the US Seventh Cavalry, one of several Irish officers serving with the United States Army who died alongside George Armstrong Custer in the Battle of the Little Bighorn. At the time of the Easter Rising, she was working as a nurse at the SDU on James Street, a cluster of mid-nineteenth century workhouses, infirmaries and churches for the capital's permanently destitute or ill. Over 3200 men and women lived and worked in the complex of mismatched buildings, streets, alleys and courtyards which stretched out over some 50 acres of land on the south-western outskirts of the city center. It has been described as a miniature, self-contained village (part of the site is now given over to the modern St. James's Hospital).

Its location was of strategic importance to the insurrection as it covered the western approaches to the capital and the proposed headquarters of the Provisional Government of the Irish Republic in the GPO building. Consequently the 120 volunteers under Commandant Éamonn Ceannt of the 4th Battalion, Dublin Brigade, of the newly formed Irish Republican Army, garrisoned themselves on the site, barricading local approaches and several structures on the grounds, including the Nurses' Home, the Female Chronic Hospital, the Protestant Hospital, and the Acute Hospital.

Although some popular histories and articles on the Rising (including Wikipedia) list her as a rebel participant and a member of Cumann na mBan, the women's auxiliary to the Irish Volunteers, Keogh was simply a nurse. She was buried on the Union Ground that evening with a short prayer, after which Commandant Ceannt referred to her as the "first martyr of the Rising."[24] Weeks later her body was exhumed and brought home to her native parish for Christian burial.

The first actual combatant killed on Easter Monday was the handsome and well-loved actor, Sean Connolly. A captain in the Irish Citizen Army, Connolly led the takeover of City Hall. Dr. Kathleen Lynn attended him in his last moments before she herself was captured by the British.

Like Molly Childers and Margaret Skinnider, Dr. Lynn also kept a journal. While hers is sketchy (she was more focused on being a physician than a historical narrator of events), we nevertheless

---

[24] Donal Fallon, "Nurse Margaret Keogh, the first civilian fatality of the Rising" (*Independent*.ie, Mar. 4 2016, https://www.independent.ie/irish-news/1916/the-victims/nurse-margaret-keogh-the-first-civilian-fatality-of-the-rising-34510459.html, accessed Sep. 25, 2021).

Fig. 12. Photograph of Margaret Keogh by Miles Keogh.

gain some insights into both the death of Sean Connolly, as well as how she and the other Irish prisoners at City Hall were treated by the British soldiers.

On Easter Monday morning, Captain Connolly was about to leave for Liberty Hall. His commander, Commandant-General James Connolly in whose play "*Under Which Flag* in the Abbey Theatre Sean had recently played a starring role, approached him to give him his final instructions. He shook his hand and said, "Good luck, Sean! We won't meet again."

Later that morning Captain Connolly and his 20 men took over Dublin Castle, shooting a police officer and then tying up six sentries in the guard room. Their mission was to delay the British

Fig. 13. Sean Connolly, ca. 1915.

reinforcements in order to give the Volunteers time to set up headquarters in the GPO. A British Army major fired at Connolly, then
went to gather more soldiers to fend off the rebels. Connolly and
his men, believing there were more troops either in or close to the
Castle, retreated to City Hall. He had the keys to that facility from
his former job as a city clerk. When his men took over that facility, they went to the roof where he and his men intended to raise
the Irish flag, the same one he had carried on stage in the Abbey
Theatre. As Connolly approached, he was shot by a sniper located
on the roof of Dublin Castle just across the way. Dr. Lynn wrote in
her journal:

We noticed Sean Connolly coming towards us, walking upright, although we had been advised to crouch and take cover as much as possible. We suddenly saw him fall mortally wounded by a sniper's bullet from the castle. First aid was useless. He died almost immediately.

Helena Molony, who also witnessed his death, later told of how his 15-year-old brother stood by the body and, crying bitterly, whispered a prayer over his older sibling.

Fig. 14. Dr. Kathleen Lynn, ca. 1914.

9

DR. KATHLEEN LYNN

K athleen Lynn was born in County Mayo to an upper middle-class family. Although she was from a family of means she witnessed the poverty and degradation of ordinary people in Ireland in the aftermath of the Famine and determined that she would be in the healing profession. She graduated from Catholic University Medical School in Dublin (later the USD School of Medicine) in 1899, then went to the US for postgraduate work, passed the board examinations there, and worked in America for a decade. Returning to Ireland, she became a fellow of the Royal College of Physicians in 1909 but was refused a position at the Adelaide General Hospital because of her gender. She was finally able to get work at two smaller hospitals, and so impressed her male supervisors that in 1910 she was recommended to be the first woman resident at the Royal Victoria Eye and Ear Hospital in Dublin. It was a position she would hold until the Rising in 1916.[25]

She was active in social work, volunteering in soup kitchens in Dublin during the 1913 lockout. She was also a suffragist and worked to secure the vote for women as a member of the executive committee of the Irish Women's Suffrage and Local Government Association. Appalled by the working conditions in Ireland, especially for women in the textile factories, she became a committed socialist. Strongly influenced by James Connolly and Constance Markiewicz, she saw the nationalist cause as the only real remedy to the suffering and injustice visited upon the Irish working class. She joined the Citizen Army and, after training members of the Cumann na mBam in emergency medical procedures, was appoint-

---

[25] "Lynn, Kathleen (1874-1955) physician and political activist," Oxford Dictionary of Medical Biography

ed by Connolly and Pearse as the Chief Medical Officer. She also trained Rosie Hackett as a medical assistant and Hackett, along with Helena Molony, were with her at the City Hall when the British overcame their small force. With the death of Connolly, she was the ranking officer when they surrendered, and described herself as "a Red Cross doctor and belligerent."[26] The later designation ensured that she would not receive any privileges because of her profession.

In her diary she kept a concise account of the daily privations and humiliations of their captivity. There were lice, fleas and generally unsanitary conditions in the overcrowded rooms where she and the other prisoners were kept. Rations were pitifully scarce and cold. She was kept in custody in Dublin until early June when she was deported to England.[27]

Among those captured at the same time was 16-year-old Molly O'Reilly[28] who hoisted the old green and gold flag of ancient Ireland over Liberty Hall on Palm Sunday[29] at the request of James Connolly, who remembered her spunk from the Dublin lockdown when she carried messages and helped run soup kitchens for the workers' dependents at the age of just 13.[30] She had first met Connolly when she was nine and was attending Irish dancing classes at Liberty Hall. She heard him speak about the workers' republic and was fascinated. Mollie marched with the ICA to take the Castle and, when the rebels retreated to City Hall, she worked as a courier until City Hall was captured and she was imprisoned with the rest.

The second civilian shooting was near St. Stephen's Green and this time by an Irish Volunteer. The accounts vary. In the most trust-

---

[26] Sadhbh Walsh, "Eight Women of the Easter Rising." *The New York Times*, Mar. 16, 2016.

[27] "The Revolutionary Diaries of Kathleen Lynn" on RCPI.ie (https://www.rcpi.ie/heritage-centre/1916-2/revolutionary-diary-kathleen-lynn/, accessed Mar. 1, 2021).

[28] Some sources put her age at 14 at the time of the flag raising in 1916. However, according to family records she was born in 1900, so those sources are incorrect. She would have been 16.

[29] "Connolly Irish Flag Proclamation" on *Marxists.org* (https://www.marxists.org/archive/connolly/1916/04/irshflag.htm, accessed Mar. 2, 2021).

[30] Mary Smith, "Women of the Easter Rising", *Rebel*, Apr. 12, 2020 (https://www.rebelnews.ie/2020/04/12/women-of-the-easter-rising/, accessed Sep. 25, 2021).

ed one, it appears that the Volunteers were attempting to establish a secure perimeter around St. Stephen's Green by setting up a barrier with commandeered vehicles. Before they could complete the task, one person belligerently refused to cooperate and was shot in the ensuing struggle. According to one witness:

> Upon my return I found our men entrenching themselves in St. Stephen's Green.
> All carried tools with which to dig themselves in, and shrubbery was used to protect the trenches. Motorcars and drays passing the Green were commandeered, too, to form a barricade. Much to the bewilderment of their occupants who had no warning that anything was amiss in Dublin, these men in green uniforms would signal them to stop. Except in one instance, they did so quickly enough. They were told to get out and an experienced chauffeur among our men would jump in at once and drive the car to a position where it was needed. The occupant would stand for a moment aghast. One drayman refused his cart and persisted in his refusal, not believing it when our men told him that this was war. He was shot.[31]

Meanwhile back at the GPO, two troops of British cavalry were dispatched from Marlborough Barracks, proceeded down Sackville Street and began to disperse the crowds gathering in the street. As they passed Nelson's Pillar, level with the GPO, the rebels opened fire, killing three cavalrymen and two horses, and fatally wounding a fourth man. The cavalry retreated and were withdrawn to their barracks. Sometime later a bomb was detonated in Phoenix Park, killing a bystander but failing to destroy the British arsenal. On Mount Street a group of reserve British soldiers came upon a rebel position and were shot and killed before they managed to retreat back to their barracks. In addition, eight of the Dublin Metropolitan Police were shot and three died, and a decision was made by their

---

[31] Skinnider (2016), 164-167.

chief to take all police off the street. That decision, unfortunately, would result in widespread looting.

Some sources credit Constance Markiewicz with the death of one of these Dublin policemen, but this has been disputed. Seven months after the Rising, in November 1916, Constance told her sister, Eva, "how she held a revolver at a policeman's chest but could not shoot when it came to the point" because "she recognized him & had known him before."[32]

Another notable encounter involving the countess did occur in the late afternoon as she patrolled in the company of a sympathetic local official. British troops from Portobello Barracks had been sent out twice to attack the rebel positions in St. Stephen's Green, before they were completely entrenched. Several rebels were shot in this attack. This to some extent explains the shooting of the drayman who had interfered with their effort to protect themselves. The second time, the Volunteers were ready and two British soldiers were shot and then abandoned by their comrades who fled the scene. According to an observer

> When it was beginning to grow dusk...I saw British soldiers coming up Harcourt Street. The countess [Markiewicz] and Town Counselor Partridge came to a halt on the street just ahead of me. The countess stood motionless, waiting for them to come near. She was a lieutenant in the Irish Volunteers and, in her officer's uniform and black hat with great plumes, looked most impressive. At length she raised her gun to her shoulder—it was an automatic over a foot long, which she had converted into a short rifle by taking the wooden holster and using it as a stock —and took aim. Neither she nor Partridge noticed me as I came up behind them. I was quite close when they fired. The shots rang out at the same moment, and I saw two officers leading the column drop to the street. As the countess was taking aim again, the soldiers, without firing a shot, turned and ran in great confusion back to the barracks.

[32] Lauren Arrington, "Did Constance Markievicz Shoot the Policeman?", on the Conference of Irish Historians in Britain website (http://irishhistoriansinbritain.org/?p=18, accessed Jan. 16, 2021).

The whole company fled as fast as they could from two people, one of them a woman![33]

The weapon referred to was commonly called 'Peter the Painter' (after an anarchist terrorist who used one in turn-of-the-century London). It was a C96 Mauser automatic pistol, one of several which were imported for the Rising. It was a clip-fed semi-automatic weapon that held ten 7.63 rounds, although some were also chambered for 9 mm. It could be equipped with a shoulder stock to make it more accurate and proved lethally effective in close-quarters street fighting during Easter Week. Later, at Mount Street Bridge, Mick Malone, armed with a C96 and accompanied by a mere 12 Volunteers, killed or wounded 240 Sherwood Foresters. Malone himself in one charge shot down ten British soldiers with his automatic pistol before taking up a Howth Mauser.

Also referred to by the Irish as the "Broomhandle," the Mauser pistol-carbine, when used with the distinctive shoulder stock holster, was the most notable of handguns used in Ireland. While it is not known how many of these pistols were carried in the uprising, at least three instances of their use have secured them a place in Irish history; the two noted above, and the courageous defense by Pádraic Pearse, the leader of the Rising, who used his to ward off the British at the GPO siege.[34]

Countess Markiewicz also carried a .455 Smith & Wesson revolver, as well as a small .32-cal. S&W revolver. She would later use her infamous "Broomhandle" again to great effect when she helped silence a British machine gun crew on the roof of the nearby Shelbourne Hotel.

---

[33] Skinnider (2016), loc. 707-713.
[34] "Guns of the Easter Rising", *American Rifleman* (https://www.americanrifleman.org/articles/2016/3/17/guns-of-the-easter-rising/, accessed Jan. 20, 2021).

Fig. 15. The C96 Mauser pistol. Also called "Peter the Painter" or "The Broomhandle."

10

MAJOR TACTICAL ERRORS
PROVE COSTLY

The failure to take Dublin Castle, the Shelbourne Hotel, and Trinity College were significant tactical errors made on the first day of the insurrection. British soldiers stationed in Dublin Castle, the center of British rule in Ireland, had gone to Fairyhouse racecourse to enjoy the Irish Grand National, leaving the city short of troops when the Rising began.

The Commander-in-Chief of the British Army in Ireland, General Lovick Friend, was on leave in England; the officer commanding the Dublin Garrison, Colonel Kennard, could not be located and it was left to his adjutant, Colonel H. V. Cowan, to call for Marlborough Barracks to investigate the disturbance at the GPO. He also called Portobello Barracks, Richmond Barracks, the Royal Barracks, and the barracks in the Curragh to send reinforcements.

Despite the absence of troops at Dublin Castle, the rebels hesitated to take the building, a move that would have been a major blow to the British, interrupting communications and also protecting the Volunteers at Jacob's Factory. The unit disarmed those in the guardroom and shot a police sentry but failed to press any further as those inside – alerted by the shots – began to close the castle gates. There were only seven British soldiers in the garrison. Instead of forcing their way past them and occupying the Castle, the small detachment of men under Captain Sean Connolly opted to leave and take City Hall instead.

The rebels also failed to take the Shelbourne Hotel just north of St. Stephen's Green which was a major tactical error. British troops would later occupy the upper reaches of this building and enfilade rebel positions with machine guns and snipers. Rebels also failed to take Trinity College Dublin which had no garrison at all and was defended by a handful of students who were later reinforced by ANZAC troops on leave from the British Army.

The sketch below clearly shows the locations of the two forces and the gaps left in the defenses of the Irish insurgents.

Easter Rising 1916

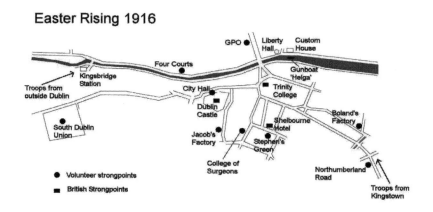

Map #3. Major conflict locations during the Easter Rising 1916.

Another obvious flaw in the defense of the city was the lack of fortifications on the banks of the Liffey River. This would allow the gunboat HMY *Helga* free passage to be in a position to shell the GPO.

It should be kept in mind that the Irish leadership did not believe that the British would shell the city of Dublin. They felt that the architecture was something the British valued and the important buildings would be safe. They also felt that token resistance would prove sufficient, and that the British would come to the negotiation table. They did not believe that there would be any major retaliation against the leaders of the insurrection since they were in uniform and should be considered combatants and protected under the universal rules of warfare. They were mistaken.

DAY TWO - TUESDAY, APRIL 26

Late Monday evening and early Tuesday morning, British reinforcements arrived and took over the Shelbourne Hotel. They installed snipers at various locations and set up a machine gun on the roof. By 4am they were raining rapid fire down on the exposed positions of the rebels in St. Stephen's Green. The garrison returned fire, but it was no use; the park offered little protection from attack. It was decided to retreat to the safety of the nearby College of Surgeons. Countess Markiewicz began to prepare the men and women for the evacuation.

Fig. 16. View of the Shelbourne Hotel from St. Stephen's Green.

They crawled along using the railings as cover, then crossed the street in small groups under cover of fire from their comrades on the rooftops. They finally made it across York Street and entered the College of Surgeons.[35]

At this time one of the most notable women warriors, Margaret Skinnider, made her appearance, first as an armed courier riding a bicycle back and forth between fortified positions, and later as a sniper. She recorded much of the action in her book, *Doing My Bit for Ireland,* a lively and highly readable memoir of the Rising.

[35] Testimony of Paddy Buttner, "I Woke Up and Heard the Machine Gun Fire" on 1916.RTE.ie (https://1916.rte.ie/relevant-places/i-woke-up-and-heard-the-machine-gun-fire/, accessed Jan. 16, 2021).

11

MARGARET SKINNIDER-
A LITERARY WARRIOR

Commandant Mallin sent me with a dispatch to headquarters. He recognized immediately that a regiment could not hold the Green against a machine-gun on a tall building that could rake our position easily. As I rode along on my bicycle, I had my first taste of the risks of street-fighting. Soldiers on the top of the Hotel Shelbourne aimed their machine-gun directly at me. Bullets struck the wooden rim of my bicycle wheel, puncturing it; others rattled on the metal rim or among the spokes. I knew one might strike me at any moment so I rode as fast as I could. My speed saved my life, and I was soon out of range around a corner.[36]

Fig. 17. Lewis Machine Gun[37]

---

[36] Skinnider (2016), loc 745-747.
[37] The Lewis Gun, .303 caliber, was light and could be carried by one person, accompanied by an ammunition bearer. The pan magazine on top held 47 or 96 rounds and was quickly interchangeable. It was highly effective against the rebels and a deciding factor in the British suppression of the Rising.

Born to Irish parents in Coatbridge, Scotland, Margaret Frances Skinnider was educated to be a mathematics teacher. She joined Cumann na mBan (Irish Women's Council) in Glasgow and was active in the women's suffrage movement. She learned how to shoot at a gun club that was originally formed to train women in Scotland to help defend Great Britain in case of invasion.

During her frequent visits to Ireland, she befriended Constance Markiewicz and became active in smuggling detonators and fuses for explosive devices into Ireland, as well as becoming quite expert in putting them together. From time to time, she helped the countess with the rifle training of Fianna Éireann, since she was an expert shot. She was supportive of the workers' union and their struggle. Prior to the Rising she actually lived in the Markiewicz home on Leinster Road.

Although she began her participation in the Rising as a scout and messenger, the Countess convinced Commander Mallin that Skinnider's specialized skills should be put to use. Subsequently, she became involved in planting explosives and incendiary devices at various locations controlled by the British, including an armory. In addition, she commanded a four-man sniper team which concentrated on removing the threat of machine gun fire from the British emplacement.

Fearless under fire, she would be shot three times during the conflict as she tried to cut off the retreat of British soldiers who had planted a machine gun nest on the roof of a church, when her team dislodged them.

As the struggle of Day 2 continued at St. Stephen's Green, many poor Dubliners descended on the area of Sackville Street and broke into the city's shops and boutiques. Some of the women stole dresses, fans, and jewelry from the shops and paraded around in the stolen finery. The police had withdrawn after a number of them were shot the previous day. The Volunteers in and around the GPO tried to enforce order and at various points discharged their weapons, firing over the heads of the looters to discourage them but were mostly unsuccessful. According to one eyewitness:

Fig. 18 & 19. Margaret Skinnider. Above, a formal photo. Below, one where she is dressed as a boy, a disguise she adopted when bicycling as a courier and messenger.

Once one shop had gone there was no halting the destruction. Quickly two others were broken into, the noise of their crashing plate glass sounded all the louder because of the new and awful stillness that had fallen over the city. Guttersnipes ran out of Dunns', the hatters, decked out in silk hats, straw hats and bowlers...

Suddenly, with a tremendous crash, the plate glass front of Boblet's, a confectioner's on the corner of Sackville Street, crashed onto the pavement. Sweets spilled out in a cascade, and men, women and children dived to the ground to scoop up handfuls of chocolate, Turkish delight, glacier mints, and fruit bon-bons.

The Civil Head of local government, Lord Lieutenant Womborne, declared martial law and handed over power to Brigadier General William Lowe. General Lowe, with 1,600 men, commenced to throw a cordon of troops around the main rebel strongholds. By mid-afternoon, St. Stephen's Green was littered with corpses, although the main rebel force had successfully retreated to the College of Surgeons where most of the wounded were being treated. With Lowe's contingent came Maxim machine guns which would have a suppressing effect on the rebels.

In the northwest, the British brought an 18-pounder field artillery piece to destroy the barricades set up by the rebels on the North Circular Road. After lengthy resistance and several casualties, the rebels withdrew from that position.

Faced with surprising resistance, Howe was to continue to increase the force used against the rebels. Added to the two light machine guns seen on the roof of the Shelbourne, he would place Maxim machine guns used at various points of rebel resistance. Also, as noted, heavy field artillery would be used to shatter barricades and ultimately reduce to rubble many buildings in the central part of the city.

Pearse, realizing that looting and lack of citizen cooperation in the city center was hampering the resistance, decided to issue a proclamation calling for a united citizen front. Some Dubliners had actually jeered the rebels whom they felt should have joined the 140,000 Irishmen who were in British uniforms fighting in the trenches against Germany. Others just wanted to go about their business and make a profit and not have their shops destroyed by looters or by British artillery. Still others, mainly slum dwellers and young delinquents, were taking advantage of the chaos to fill their carts with stolen goods from unguarded shops. Pearse read his manifesto at the foot of Nelson's Pillar in midafternoon.

THE PROVISIONAL GOVERNMENT To The CITIZENS OF DUBLIN
The Provisional Government of the Irish Republic salutes the Citizens of Dublin on the momentous occasion of the proclamation of a SOVEREIGN INDEPENDENT IRISH STATE, now in course of being established by Irishmen in arms.

The Republican forces hold the lines taken up at twelve noon on Easter Monday, and nowhere, despite fierce and almost continuous attacks of the British troops, have the lines been broken through. The country is rising in answer to Dublin's call, and the final achievement of Ireland's freedom is now, with God's help, only a matter of days. The valour, self-sacrifice and discipline of Irish men and women are about to win for our country a glorious place among the nations.

Ireland's honour has already been redeemed; it remains to vindicate her wisdom and her self-control. All citizens of Dublin who believe in the right of their country to be free will give their allegiance and their loyal help to the Irish Republic. There is work for everyone: for the men in the fighting line, and for the women in the provision of food and first aid. Every Irishman and Irishwoman worthy of the name will come forward to help their common country in this her supreme hour. Able-bodied citizens can help by building barricades in the streets to oppose the advance of the British troops. The British troops have been firing on our women and on our Red Cross. On the other hand, Irish Regiments in the British Army have refused to act against their fellow-countrymen.

The Provisional Government hopes that its supporters which means the vast bulk of the people of Dublin—will preserve order and self-restraint. Such looting as has already occurred has been done by hangers-on of the British Army. Ireland must keep her new honour unsmirched. We have lived to see an Irish Republic proclaimed. May we live to establish it firmly, and may our children and our children's children enjoy the happiness and prosperity which freedom will bring.

Signed on behalf of the Provisional Government, P. H. PEARSE,

Commanding in Chief of the Forces of the Irish Republic, and President of the Provisional Government.

One can observe in Pearse's manifesto the secondary role he appeared to assign to women. He was a conservative in the matter. James Connolly, the military commander of the Citizen Army, had no such reservations. And it was Connolly who did most of the military planning and strategic maneuvering and assured that women had a more equal role. It was Connolly who goaded Pearse and Clarke to strike immediately before Irish youth were conscripted to serve in the British Army. "I know of no foreign enemy of this country," he said, "except the British Government."[38]

By 4pm additional soldiers from the 25th Irish Reserve Infantry Battalion and other units had joined General Lowe's troops. By the end of the day there would be almost 7,000 British troops facing about 1,600 rebels. In addition, the reinforcements had brought with them the more powerful Vickers machine guns, and 18-pounder artillery batteries.

38 James Connolly, "What Should Irish People Do During the War?", originally published Aug. 8, 1914 in the *Irish Worker*, RTE https://www.rte.ie/centuryireland/index.php/articles/james-connolly-what-should-irish-people-do-during-the-war, (Accessed Jan. 16, 2021).

12

HELENA MOLONY, ACTRESS AND REBEL

B ack at City Hall, actress and rebel fighter Helena Molony and her comrades had been under constant attack from both machine guns and artillery. Ultimately the defenders were overrun and forced to surrender. Maloney and the other women were taken to a barracks room at Dublin Castle and imprisoned.

Fig. 20. Helena Molony, 1916 lithograph.

Since Molony and her comrades at City Hall would be imprisoned for the remainder of the conflict, it is appropriate that we pause to share her background and contributions and not simply pass her by as previous historians have done. Orphaned as a young girl, she spent many hours alone reading about the legends and history of Ireland. Hearing the famous actress Maud Gonne speaking in Dublin one night she was inspired to take part in the cultural revival that was sweeping Ireland at the turn of the century. She joined a group called the Daughters of Ireland (Inghinidhe na hÉireann) and boycotted the visit of Queen Victoria to Dublin in 1900. In her twenties she became more socially active and radical, organizing Irish classes for poor children, campaigning for school meals, pressuring shops to carry Irish goods not British imports, and discouraging the recruitment of Irish boys into the British Army. A committed agitator and speaker, she had many contacts with the police.

Like James Connolly she was an early convert to socialism, feminism, and Irish nationalism. She founded a feminist newspaper that was to have a major influence on the thinking and subsequent radicalization of both Countess Markiewicz and Dr. Kathleen Lynn. She visited Markiewicz often at her home and helped her train the boys in the Fianna Éirann.[39] Connolly became aware of her work when he read her column "Labor Notes." Through him she began to see that Irish nationalism and socialism were not separate ideas but a single one. She came to realize that global capitalism was just another form of imperialism and could not be separated from the independence movement. Independence without a change in the economic structure, it became clear, would just be a change of masters. As Connolly put it:

> The cry for a union of classes is in reality an insidious move on the part of our Irish master class to have the powers of government transferred from the hands of the English capitalist government to the hands of an Irish capitalist government and to pave the way for this change by

---

[39] Fearghal McGarry, "Helena Molony: A Revolutionary Life", *History Ireland* (https://www.historyireland.com/18th-19th-century-history/helena-molony-a-revolutionary-life/, accessed Jan. 17, 2021).

inducing the Irish worker to abandon all hopes of bettering his own position.[40]

Drawing on her skills as an Abbey actor, she led women in support of the 1913 Dublin lockout. Most amusingly, she borrowed a makeup kit from the backstage of the theater and disguised firebrand Jim Larkin (who was wanted by the authorities for being a known agitator) as an elderly clergyman so that he could give his famous speech at the Imperial Hotel without the police knowing it was him. She addressed strike meetings and helped organize the food kitchen in Liberty Hall, which took care of the strikers' most pressing needs. After a brief illness (most likely a collapse from overwork) and recuperation in France with Maud Gonne,[41] she returned to Ireland and became general secretary of the Irish Women Workers Union (IWWU) and manager of the worker's co-op in Liberty Hall. She also trained girls for Connolly's Irish Citizen Army and went about always armed with a revolver.

Now, just as the Rising was heating up, she was captured and placed under guard. Captured at City Hall, she was to spend the remainder of Easter Week imprisoned in a dirty room without facilities in the Ship Street barracks. The following week she was transported to Kilmainham Gaol where she would hear the firing squads killing the rebel leaders. She witnessed her friend and mentor James Connolly being dragged out, terribly wounded and unable to stand, and then tied to a chair to be shot. She considered it murder, plain and simple. After that, she said, "life seemed to have come to an end for me."[42]

---

[40] James Connolly (author) and Shaun Harkin (ed.), *A James Connolly Reader* (Chicago: Haymarket Books, 2018).

[41] Maud Gonne will be referenced from time to time in this book. Although she was in Paris at the time of the Rising, she influenced many of the Rising leaders and cultural icons of her day. She was an ardent nationalist, a famous actress, and the muse of poet William Butler Yeats who proposed marriage to her on four separate occasions. She was married but separated from Major John MacBride, a leader in the Rising who was subsequently executed and is referenced in Yeats' famous poem "Easter 1916" in an uncomplimentary way. (See Appendix C).

[42] Quoted in *History Ireland*, cf. note 14.

13

THE MURDER OF A PACIFIST

On Sackville (O'Connell) Street there was only sporadic fire. However, looters continued to run amuck, smashing the windows of jewelry stores and high-end clothiers, lighting fires, selling stolen diamond rings and other items. Children looted Lawrence's Toy Shop and stole fireworks which they set off in the street, creating pandemonium.

Throughout the rest of the city women had been accepted in the ranks of all the rebel units with the exception of Eamon de Valera's battalion. Even Pearse's headquarters now had women participating under arms. The buttoned-down de Valera, however, would have none of it. With his troops stationed in Boland's Mill, he refused to countenance the idea of women combatants. A group of women from Cumann na mBan had assembled in Merrion Square ready to receive orders from him, but none arrived.

In response to the reports of looting, Francis Sheehy-Skeffington, a pacifist and well-known local figure, went to the city center to attempt to prevent it. However, he was arrested at Portobello Bridge by members of the 11th East Surrey Regiment and fell into the hands of the most notoriously unbalanced of British officers, Captain J.C. Bowen-Colthurst. Poor Francis was at first merely held hostage by an army raiding party and, per Bowen-Colthurst's orders, kept prisoner along with two journalists who had the misfortune to be in a shop the troop raided.[43]

However, the following morning at around 10.20, having spent much of the night reading the Bible, Captain Bowen-Colthurst went

---

[43] Sheila Langan, Frances Mulraney, and Kate Hickey, "On This Day: Ireland's Easter Rising begins in 1916", *Irish Central*, Apr. 24, 2021 (https://www.irishcentral.com/roots/history/timeline-irelands-1916-easter-rising, accessed Jan. 17, 2021).

to the Guardroom and told the duty officer, an 18-year-old second lieutenant, that "he was going to take out three prisoners and shoot them, as he thought it was the right thing to do."[44] The three were brought into an enclosed yard where Bowen-Colthurst assembled a firing squad from the guard, ordering them to load, aim and fire. The three fell fatally wounded and, when movement was seen, the captain ordered Second Lieutenant Dobbin to form another firing squad and fire again. Following this, by all accounts, the agitated and excited Captain Bowen-Colthurst took a party of troops ostensibly to attack rebel positions in the city. Unverified accounts claim that during this enterprise, the captain shot at least two other unarmed civilians in cold blood.[45]

Unaware that Francis had been executed, his wife Hanna continued with her work delivering messages and bringing food to the rebel troops at the General Post Office. Like her husband, Hanna had been active in anti-recruiting activities, but more recently had been persuaded by James Connolly of the importance of supporting the Rising.

Hanna was born in Kanturk, County Cork to a large but prosperous family. Her father was an MP for the Irish Parliamentary Party. Both she and her brother were close friends with James Joyce and the family lived next door to the Lord Mayor of Dublin. Joyce introduced her to her future husband, and they married in their graduation gowns, Hanna having received an MA from the Royal University of Ireland with first class honors. They agreed to take each other's last names as a sign of equality.

She was persuaded by James Connolly to the socialist cause during the Dublin lockout and had long been a nationalist, as was

---

[44] Ibid.

[45] Michael Nugent, "Captain John Bowen-Colthurst", *WW1 Research Ireland* (https://ww1researchireland.com/captain-john-bowen-colthurst/, accessed Jan. 17, 2021).Ultimately the captain would be court-martialed by the British Army for these murders. Because of injuries suffered in combat in World War I, however, and several other examples of irrational behavior, he was found to be insane and committed to Broadmoor Hospital. He was released in 1918 and moved to Vancouver, BC where his family had an estate.

her father and the rest of her family. She fought to obtain the right for women to vote and was elected as president of the Irish Women's Franchise League. She and Francis were co-founders of *The Irish Citizen*, one of the first feminist newspapers in Ireland, and had both been arrested for anti-recruiting activities in 1915.

Francis was also an early proponent of women's rights before he met Hanna. He often wore a "Votes for Women" badge at the university where he was well known for his nonconformist attitude, refusing to shave and wearing knickerbocker socks instead of straight pants. He was the model for a colorful university character in Joyce's *A Portrait of an Artist as a Young Man*.

He was friends with Constance Markiewicz as well and supported her when she was arrested for her anti-recruitment activities. Unlike the Countess, however, he deplored violence and considered himself a pacifist. While he was a supporter of the nationalist cause, he refused to be a combatant. So his death was a particularly disheartening tragedy. He had first appeared on Sackville Street when he saw a British soldier shot and tried to come to his aid. Later, when he saw a crowd looting stores, he tried to discourage them. They reacted with shouts, mostly good-natured hoots, since they knew him from his various protests around the city. But British soldiers, mistaking him as a leader of the crowd and a revolutionary, arrested and summarily executed him without even a hearing. When she learned of his execution Countess Markiewicz exclaimed, "Why on earth did they shoot Skeffy? He didn't believe in violence."[46]

As day two of the Rising came to an end, things were a bit challenging for the rebels. But Pearse, Connolly, and others put a brave face to it. One commented that they had already outlasted Robert Emmet, whose Rebellion of 1803 was suppressed after two hours. They had not been betrayed by any of their men or women. They still held most of the important defensive positions in and around Dublin. They had not suffered any major defeat. Except for one

---

[46] Lauren Arrington, *Revolutionary Lives: Constance and Casimir Markiewicz* (Princeton: Princeton University Press, 2016), 145-146.

Fig. 21. Francis and Hanna Sheehy-Skeffington, ca. 1915. Photographer unknown.

small portion of the Union, and the City Hall, none of their men or women had to give up a position or were captured. While they were forced to retreat from St. Stephen's Green, they still held the College of Surgeons, and the British now knew that they were up against a formidable force.

The British, without informants or other intelligence, could not know that they were facing a force of less than 1,500. Nor could they know whether rebel forces from other parts of Ireland might arrive at any moment, or if the Germans—seeing that the Empire's forces were tied down in the capitol—might invade in support of the rebels. Some even thought that Irish Americans might have been recruited. As a result, General Lowe and his staff would wait for more reinforcements before making tactical troop movements.

14

FIRST RADIO BROADCAST, NEW RIFLES, AND FAKE NEWS

The British had cut all telephone and telegraph lines, so the rebels had no way of communicating with the outside world. However, Commandant Joseph Plunkett had an idea. Across the street at the Wireless School of Telegraphy, which the British had abandoned, there might be some way of communicating. He sent seven men, including a radio technician named Johnny O'Connor, to see what could be done. He gave them a message written by James Connolly to transmit to the world press.

> Irish Republic declared in Dublin today. Irish troops have captured the city and are in full possession. Enemy cannot move. Whole country is rising. [47]

It was intended to be a transmission sent to a fixed point in Cahersiveen and then on to America but there was no place to transmit to because the receiver at the other end was not operating. It could not be sent by telegraph because the wires were down. O'Connor climbed up the wireless mast, braving sniper fire the whole time, and repaired the antenna. Meanwhile Marconi operator David Burke broadcast the message in Morse Code, even though he knew it could not go far. Both men hoped it might be picked up by nearby

---

[47] "Irish Republic Declared: Historic Radio Broadcast Re-enacted", *The Irish Times*, Apr. 25, 2016 (https://www.irishtimes.com/news/ireland/irish-news/irish-republic-declared-historic-radio-broadcast-re-enacted-1.2624118, accessed April 25, 2021).

ships and then transmitted onwards.[48] Thus, it was the first "radio broadcast" in history. He repeated the message at timed intervals for several hours throughout the night. Ultimately, it was picked up by ships at sea and sent on to America and other locations including Spain and Poland.

At 8.15pm the British gun yacht HMY *Helga* entered the Liffey River and began firing at Boland's Mills, damaging an upper story and forcing the rebels from the sniper positions. In addition, heavy artillery was moved into the Phibsborough area and Trinity College. This additional firepower would prove overwhelming. James Connolly always believed that the British would never destroy the impressive buildings of the "Empire's second city." He would be proven wrong.

Tuesday evening was chilly with a slight breeze and intermittent showers. The rebels, before hunkering down for the night, reinforced their hold on Sackville Street and set up firing teams in both the Imperial and Metropole Hotels.

Back at the Royal College of Surgeons near St. Stephen's Green, Countess Markiewicz discovered a cache of 67 Lee-Enfield rifles with 15,000 rounds of ammunition, as well as bandoliers and haversacks. These belonged to the training corps and would have been used against the rebels had they not taken the building. These rifles were far superior to the Howth Mausers in that they used smokeless powder which would not give away the rebels' positions, and were more accurate. Commandant Mallin passed them out and ordered sharpshooters to go up to the roof of the College where they could snipe at the machine gunners firing from the Shelbourne Hotel.

The Howth Rifle with which most of the rebels were equipped was properly called the Mauser, model 1871. It was a cheap but obsolete rifle. It got its name in Ireland from Howth Harbor in County Dublin where 1500 of the rifles were landed after being smuggled from Germany in 1914 by Erskine and Molly Childers and

---

[48] The site of the Wireless School of Telegraphy, which was destroyed by the British, is now occupied by the Grand Central Café in Lower O'Connell Street. A popular eatery and pub.

Mary Spring Rice. They were single-shot rifles, firing an 11mm black powder cartridge, and in terms of firearms development were a generation behind the weapons used by the British Army in Dublin in 1916. They had a very heavy kick and, as noted, the black powder smoke gave away the position of the shooter before he or she had a chance to reload.

Fig. 22. Mauser Rifle, Model 1871.

The Lee-Enfield, on the other hand, was up-to-date and accurate, as well as capable of much more rapid fire. Some of these were obtained by the rebels in the months before the Rising usually through bribing British soldiers into claiming their rifles as "lost" (the going price was five pounds sterling), while others were captured during the week-long fight. With its 10-round magazine capacity, potent Mk VII .303 British cartridge and slick action, the Lee-Enfield was one of the most useful weapons in the hands of the insurgents. The contingent at the College of Surgeons were now very well armed.

Fig. 23. Lee-Enfield rifle used by British Forces during the Easter Rising.

It was soon discovered, however, that the roof of the College was a vulnerable position. The Shelbourne was much higher and this left the rebels exposed to enemy fire from British machine gunners. When this was reported to Commandant Mallin, he ordered them to come back inside.

And so, all over Dublin, the rebels hunkered down and tried to keep warm as a cold breeze swept in from the river, and a mist settled on the roofs of towers. It would be a long, cold, and damp wait until dawn.

FAKE NEWS FROM AMERICA (VIA LONDON)

Fig. 24. Misleading headline and false news. *New York Times*, April 26, 1916.

According to the *New York Times* of Wednesday, April 26, 1916, the Irish Rising was over. "Troops Crush Revolt in Ireland; Take Post Office Seized by Rioters" screamed the bold headline on page one of the newspaper. Although there had been a few casualties ("Military Lose 12 Killed"), the paper reported, the "government says trouble is in hand and has not spread."

Well, that is the problem with trusting official government sources, in this case the War Office in London. It was wildly inaccurate and misleading. In fact, the rebels had taken over several major installations, blockaded main streets, and controlled much of central Dublin including the GPO which was their secure headquarters. In addition, Wednesday would be the bloodiest day of all for the overconfident and ill-prepared British forces.

The *New York Times Magazine* did a bit better when they finally got hold of a witness to the action. The journalist and poet Joyce Kilmer interviewed Moira Regan, a member of the Cumann na mBan who was actively working as a courier throughout the Rising. She was quite clear about the strong rebel positions. At the GPO on Tuesday, she observed several prisoners, British Army enlisted men, peeling potatoes and washing dishes for the rebel forces. The captured British officers were held in a back room. She noted:

> The rebels had captured many important buildings. They had possession of several big houses on O'Connell Street near the Post Office. They had taken the Imperial Hotel which belonged to Murphy, Dublin's great capitalist, and had turned it into a hospital. We found the kitchen well stocked with food. We made big sandwiches or beef and cheese and portioned out milk and beef tea.[49]
>
> ...We worked all Tuesday night, getting perhaps an hour's sleep with mattresses on the floor. The men were shooting from the windows of the Post Office, and the soldiers were shooting back, but not one of the men were injured. We expected that Inniskillings [British reinforcements] would move on Dublin from the north but no attack was made that night.[50]

[49] Joyce Kilmer, "Irish Girl Rebel Tells of Dublin Fighting", *The New York Times,* (Magazine Section), Aug. 20, 1916, 4.
[50] For facsimile of text see below. (Available to subscribers of the *New York Times* Archives. https://www.nytimes.com/1916/08/20/archives/irish-girl-rebel-tells-of-dublin-fighting-moira-regan-now-here.html, accessed Jan. 20, 2021.)

15
NELLIE GIFFORD, THE PROVISIONER

Fig. 25. Nellie Gifford, ca. 1896. Photographer unknown.

Nothing sets the day off better than a good breakfast. Thanks to Helen ("Nellie") Gifford, there was sufficient bread, sausage, and even fresh eggs, as well as porridge and tea for breakfast. Gifford was someone whom they had all grown dependent upon. She was a persuasive leader and an encouraging presence during the Rising. In addition to supplying food and often supervising its preparation, she also was able to convince captured British soldiers to peel potatoes and wash dishes, which most did enthusiastically.[51]

Gifford was born to a Unionist family and raised a Protestant. She attended college, received a teaching degree, and worked for several years as a rural teacher (boarding in the homes of host families) where she encountered poverty and the deplorable living conditions of the tenant farmers. She became an advocate for land reform and nationalism. Upon her return to Dublin, she became involved in workers' rights movements, and was an active participant in the Dublin lockout, risking arrest by posing as the niece of firebrand James Larkin, who was wanted by the police and in disguise. She also became active in the feminist movement, befriended Countess Markiewicz, and even acted in several plays at the Abbey Theatre.[52]

Impressed by James Connolly's commitment to feminism, she was one of the first women to join the Irish Citizen Army, trained in the use of weapons, and gave lessons on the culinary arts at Liberty Hall. On Easter Monday, she joined Countess Markiewicz on St. Stephen's Green, armed and ready for combat. Perceiving, however, the great need for provisions, she undertook to stop trucks carrying foodstuffs and impounded them for army use. She also commandeered meat, bread and milk from local shops and distributed provisions to the other garrisons and outlying posts through Easter week. These activities not only endeared her to the volunteers but were responsible in no small way for the high level of morale among the rebels during the difficult days and cold damp nights of the conflict.

[51] Skinnider, *op.cit.* loc.46. Some of them got a bit too friendly with the young women who were also helping prepare the food, according to Skinnider. Countess Markiewicz had to forcefully put her foot down and forbid fraternization! See also Joseph McKenna, *Voices of the Easter Rising: Firsthand Accounts Of Ireland's 1916 Rebellion* (Jefferson, NC: McFarland, 2017), 165.
[52] Anne Clare, *Unlikely Rebels: The Gifford Girls and the Fight for Irish Freedom* (Dublin: Mercier Press, 2011), 156.

DAY THREE - WEDNESDAY, APRIL 26.

The next morning Commandant Mallin suggested that the snipers climb up and over the rafters beneath the sloping roof of the College and cut holes directly under the roof. From there they could fire with perfect safety and without exposing themselves to the Shelbourne Hotel's machine gunners.

At this time, Countess Markiewicz noticed that Margaret Skinnider had returned from messenger service and was standing about in her civilian clothes anxious for combat. Knowing her to be an excellent shot, the Countess suggested to Mallin that Skinnider might be of some use under the roof. He gave his permission at once. As Margaret Skinnider remembered it:

> Madam had a fine uniform of green moleskin made for me. With her usual generosity she had mine made of better material than her own. It consisted of knee britches, belted coat and puttees. I slipped into this uniform, climbed up astride the rafters, and was assigned a loophole through which to shoot. It was dark there, full of smoke and the din of firing, but it was good to be in action. I could look across the tops of trees and see the British soldiers on the roof of the Shelbourne. I could also hear their shot hailing against the roof and wall of our fortress, for in truth this building was just that. More than once I saw the man I aimed at fall.[53]

She notes that to those who were following the Great War in Europe and read of the hundreds of thousands who died in a single battery in mile-long trench warfare, this exchange of fire across a Dublin green might seem like a small matter. But for us, she noted, "every shot we fired was a declaration to the world that Ireland, a small country but large in our hearts, was demanding her independence." They would indeed be shots heard round the world.

[53] Skinnider, *op. cit.* loc. 826-829.

16

A BRIEF INTERLUDE

Fig. 26. Ducks on lake, St. Stephen's Green.

M eanwhile, there was a sudden ceasefire—reminiscent of the famous incident on Christmas Eve in the Great War between the Germans and the British on the Continent. Both sides put up their rifles, and the machine guns of the British were silenced, as the caretaker of St. Stephen's Green emerged from his small cottage near Earlsfort Terrace, carrying a sack of feed for the freshwater fowl on the lovely lake which was his particular care. It was the home to mallard ducks, swans, and even moorhens. Both sides respectfully held their fire, fascinated by the scene unfolding. [54]

He slowly wound his way past the rebel emplacements, indifferent to the rifles pointed in his direction. They watched with some astonishment as he walked over to the pond and began scattering

[54] Peter DeRosa, *Rebels: The Irish Rising of 1916* (New York: Ballantine Books, 1992), 324.

the feed. The man was James Kearney, who took his responsibilities seriously and would brook no interference, gunfire be damned. And both the Citizen Army fighters and the British soldiers accorded him respect as he went about his duties.

Moreover, this would not be just a one-off event like that of the brief truce during the "War to End All Wars" on the Continent. On the contrary, Mr. Kearney would appear with his brown sack on the stoop of his caretaker's cottage each morning at 10:30 and each afternoon at 2:30, not even waiting until the bullets stopped flying before forging ahead—confident that nothing should disturb his sacred mission to feed the avian brood under his care.

But the lull was fleeting. Frustrated by rebels firing from under the roof of the College of Surgeons, the British commander ordered additional machine guns to be placed on the roofs of the United Service Club and the Alexandra Club to enfilade rebel positions.

17

THE BRITISH BRING IN HEAVY FIREPOWER

O ut on the Liffey River, HMY *Helga* shelled Liberty Hall and nearby Northumberland House. It fired a total of 24 explosive naval shells from its 12-inch naval guns. While the gunboat inflicted some damage, the rebels had already vacated Liberty Hall, so there were no direct casualties. [55]

Fig. 27. HMY *Helga* was used by the British to shell Liberty Hall and surrounding buildings.

Meanwhile at Trinity College, powerful 18-pounder artillery pieces commenced firing at Boland's Mills and then in Sackville (O'Connell) Street destroying several barricades and nearby buildings. [56] Introduced in 1904 as a result of deliberations by the Royal Artillery following the Boer War (1899-1902), the 18-pounder was a

---

[55] Michael Barry, "The Helga and the Shelling of Liberty Hall", *The Irish Story*, Mar. 24 2016 (https://www.theirishstory.com/2016/03/24/the-helga-and-the-shelling-of-liberty-hall/#.YEprL51KgdU, accessed Jan. 20, 2021.)

[56] Ibid.

heavier version of the 13-pound Horse Artillery weapon. Over 1,000 had been made by the start of World War I where it was seen as the most effective field gun. Over 8,000 were eventually manufactured during the War and between them fired 100 million shells. With a crew of ten men, it could fire 18-pound shrapnel, high explosive, or smoke shells up to six kilometers (over 6,500 yards).[57]

Fig. 28. Quick-firing 18-pounder field gun, Mark I. The most powerful piece of artillery used by the British during the Rising.

Most of the main rebel positions, including the GPO, the Four Courts, Jacob's Factory and Boland's Mills, saw little action. The British surrounded and bombarded them rather than assaulting them directly with infantry. In those places where the British tried to bring in more reinforcements, there was fierce fighting. However, the major thrust of the Empire leadership was to put heavy artillery

[57] "Quick Firing, 18-pounder Field Gun Mark 1, 1906", on National Army Museum website (https://collection.nam.ac.uk/detail.php?acc=1998-09-17-1, accessed Jan. 20, 2021.)

in position to remove the rebel barricades and reduce resistance along the main feeder routes to Sackville Street.

Hundreds of British troops also encircled the Mendicity Institution, which was occupied by 26 Volunteers under Seán Heuston. British troops advanced on the building, supported by snipers and machine-gun fire, but the Volunteers put up stiff resistance. Eventually, the troops got close enough to hurl grenades into the building, some of which the rebels threw back. Exhausted and almost out of ammunition, Heuston's men became the first rebel position to surrender. Heuston had been ordered to hold his position for a few hours, to delay the British, but had held on for three days. But the British were not the only ones to hurl grenades or plant explosives. Back at the College of Surgeons, the irrepressible Margaret Skinnider would come up with a clever but risky plan.

TIME TO TAKE THE OFFENSIVE

On Wednesday evening, after a meager ration of bread and a thin soup made with bouillon cubes, the group in the College of Surgeons were in the lecture hall taking a break now that the fighting had eased up. A group of them were singing rebel ballads including one penned by the Countess which was set to a Polish revolutionary air.

Margaret Skinnider was upstairs, frustrated that her sniper team had been unable to make much of an impact on the machine-gun emplacements on the roof of the Hotel Shelbourne. She began to brainstorm ways in which she might be able to make a difference. She was skilled in the use of explosives. She had in fact smuggled a significant amount of high explosive and fuses into Ireland from Scotland. Suddenly, she had an idea! She decided to approach Commandant Mallin with a proposal.

She went downstairs and asked him for permission to approach the Hotel Shelbourne under cover of darkness with a single escort. With the escort giving her cover she would smash the ground-floor window of the hotel and throw a bomb attached to an eight-second fuse inside. Knowing that the explosion would kill or injure some and force others to abandon their positions, it seemed like a workable idea. Mallin admired her initiative but, upon reflection, replied that it was far too dangerous and there would be little practical effect on the machine-gun emplacements since they were on the roof, and the explosion would affect only an unknown number of soldiers on the bottom floor.

Margaret replied that there would be a major resurgence in morale. She believed it would also encourage other ranks of Volunteers and Citizen Army soldiers to take the offensive. For the past three days they had been mostly assuming defensive postures and, while they had not suffered many casualties, neither had they inflicted much damage on the enemy. In addition, they were forced to retreat from several positions.

Mallin agreed with that but said that he was reluctant to let a woman take up that type of risk. To which Margaret responded that women had the same right as men to risk their lives for Ireland and that the new constitution of the Republic put them on equal footing with men. Mallin nodded in approval.

"Understood," he replied. "That being the case, I have another proposal which is even more important." He then detailed a special mission in which she would take an active role.

There was a machine-gun emplacement on the flat roof of the University Church which cut off the College of Surgeons from other commands. To isolate this position and eliminate the gun, it would be necessary to burn two buildings. Not only would it be a wise tactical move, but it would also expose the egregious violation of the rules of war which the British had committed by using the church as a stronghold. It was a rule that the rebels scrupulously respected but that the British, despite their oft-invoked demand for fair play, hypocritically ignored.

Mallin assigned Counselor Partridge, along with Margaret Skinnider and three others to burn one building, and a team of five other Citizen Army men to set fire to the second. When the first team arrived at their building Partridge smashed the glass door of the entrance with his rifle butt causing the weapon to discharge. The flash from his rifle barrel alerted British troops nearby and they fired a volley just as Skinnider rose to enter the doorway. She was shot in the back and from the side by British gunfire and fell, badly wounded. Partridge pulled her up and helped her to the street where they saw a young member of the group, Fred Ryan, lying in a pool of blood. Unfortunately, when they stopped to check on his condition, they both observed that he was dead. Weak from loss of blood, Skinnider herself collapsed in the street and Mallin called another rebel to assist in carrying her out of the line of fire. Meanwhile, the other team were successful in their attempt and managed to set fire to one of the buildings which occupied the British soldiers long enough for Mallin and Skinnider to make their escape and arrived back at the College of Surgeons.

When they arrived back at the College, Skinnider was put on an examining table and her blouse was cut away to reveal the wounds. She had been shot in three places, the right arm, the right side, and the back. A medical student in residence was able to extract the bullets after several probes and thus reduce the possibility of further complications. No vital organs had been damaged. However, there was still the danger of infection from uniform cloth and dirt which had entered the wounds. Hopefully, a doctor could be consulted soon to provide additional treatment.

But Easter Week 1916 was a decade away from the 1926 discovery of penicillin by Alexander Fleming, and the antibiotics which we know today. When a doctor was finally found who could treat the wounds, he prescribed mercuric chloride as an antiseptic treatment. Also called corrosive sublimate, it was first used by Arab physicians in the Middle Ages but still utilized by many doctors well into the twentieth century.[58] Among its side effects were painful irritation at the source of the wounds, gastrointestinal problems and liver problems associated with its toxicity, and bronchial irrita-

---

[58] A.D. Russell, W.B. Hugo, *Principles and Practice of Disinfection, Preservation and Sterilization* (Oxford: John Wiley & Sons, 2007), 4.

tion. Although she did not suffer greatly from the initial shooting, the treatment was extremely painful. In her weakened state, she also contracted pneumonia.

Fortunately, her friend the Countess returned from a successful mission. She not only had good news, but she brought salves and a young nurse to ease the pain of the corrosive "antibiotic." For a while, Margaret was delirious and moaning but when she recovered her senses, the Countess told her of her successful mission.

It seems they had gone out to where Fred Ryan lay, and Partridge, to attract the fire of the soldiers across the street in the Sinn Fein Bank and had stopped over the dead boy to lift him. There were only two soldiers and they both fired. That gave Madam a chance to sight them. She fired twice and killed both. "You are avenged, my dear."[59]

59 Skinnider, *op.cit.* loc 910.

18

MADELEINE FFRENCH (sic) MULLEN

Fighting alongside Margaret Skinnider and Countess Markiewicz at both St. Stephen's Green and the College of Surgeons was Madeleine ffrench-Mullen, a determined bulldog of a warrior whom Commandant Mallin also depended upon as a sniper and a committed soldier.

Madeleine ffrench-Mullen was the daughter of a Royal Navy Surgeon, who was also an admirer of Charles Steward Parnell, an early leader of the Irish Home Rule movement. Madeleine was raised in a household which was very political. She was an earnest advocate of an independent Ireland as well as a radical feminist, views which her parent also enthusiastically supported. She was an intimate friend of Dr. Kathleen Lynn whom she met at a meeting of the Daughters of Ireland, a radical group founded by Maud Gonne which was a forerunner of the Cumann na mBan. In 1915, they moved in together at Dr Lynn's Rathmines' home. As someone committed not only to equal rights, but also to equal responsibilities, she became an active combatant with the ICA at St. Stephen's Green and at the College of Surgeons fighting alongside Countess Markiewicz and Margaret Skinnider.

She remembers the frustration of trying to get treatment for Skinnider's bullet wounds. Unfortunately, her friend Dr. Lynn had already been captured by the British.

Spent 3 hours trying to induce Doctor to come and look at the poor girl. The British government has forbidden with such severe penalties any Doctor to aid us unless in the Hospitals where they can arrest us at leisure that it was almost impossible to get help. But at last a young doctor, a member of the recruiting committee and quite on the other side, came with me for the sake of the girl, all honour to him.[60]

When the fighting died down, she assisted with the nursing of Skinnider, and stayed with her throughout her ordeal. When it became inevitable that the College of Surgeons might fall to the British, she wrote in her journal that she had no fear of death or prison as long as her friend, Dr. Lynn, was by her side.

As to the ½ dozen men who, as orderlies, helped me with the wounded and the rations and made it possible for me to get through the work I shall never forget them. Nor do I wish to omit mention of the girls who worked so cheerfully night and day and faced fire so courageously that they made the men ashamed to flinch. In spite of the constant danger and the hardships there was a cheerful friendliness and peacefulness pervading the whole fortress which made for happiness. This was largely due to the influence of our leaders. Countess Markiewicz I already knew for many years and the admiration I had for her was hardly capable of any increase. Commandant M. Mallin I hardly knew by sight that Easter Monday when I was placed under his command but at the end of that week, I knew him better than many life acquaintances. I don't know what struck me most about the man, perhaps his wonderful patience and self-control. I have known him to work long hours without either food or sleep and yet he would never show the slightest sign of irritation under the most exasperating circumstances. He thought of everyone and everything, not merely the important matters but little details as regards our comforts that few men would even think of. With all that he kept strict discipline.[61]

[60] Madeleine ffrench-Mullen, *Transcript of Diary of Madeleine ffrench-Mullen. Written in Kilmainham and Mountjoy Jails, 5-20, 1916* (http://slinabande.ie/wordpress/wp-content/uploads/2010/01/DiaryMFM1916.pdf, accessed Jan. 22, 2021).
[61] Ibid., 7.

19

A PLEASANT LOYALIST
NEIGHBORHOOD AND FRANCES
O'FLAHERTY

Mount Street Bridge was an upscale community in Dublin with tree-lined streets and well-to-do homes. Most of the residents in the area were Loyalists who supported the British government, although their servants, the workers in the nearby Boland's Mills and various shops had less enthusiasm for their rulers.

Knowing that the British reinforcements from England would be coming by ship through the Kingstown Port, Commandant de Valera ordered Lieutenant Michael ('Mick') Malone, a 28-year-old carpenter, and Seamus Grace to take a handful of men and a couple of young boys to secure the area. They occupied buildings and blocked the windows and doors with furniture. The buildings included 25 Northumberland Road, the Parochial Hall, Clanwilliam House, and a schoolhouse. He had worked out what he felt were excellent battle plans initially but, seeing how few men he had available, curtailed most of them. Meanwhile, he set up his headquarters in Boland's Mills. His orders were to secure the Mills and the Mount Street Bridge and if possible to prevent the British from entering the city center, or at least significantly delay them. De Valera had two small garrisons, Malone's group and a backup at the schoolhouse. A total of 50 men.

Information was received by Pearse early Wednesday morning that as many as 2,000 troops would be on their way to put down the rebellion. Aware that some of these might be coming via Mount Street Bridge, James Connolly ordered Frances O'Flaherty, a messenger at the GPO, to proceed to Mount Street and pass the word to de Valera and Mick Malone. He also asked Jimmy Mahon to accompany her and to stay and help the undermanned Malone hold off the British. Malone meanwhile had sent two underaged boys in his command home to spare their lives in what he knew would be a deadly battle. At Clanwilliam House, the decision to send another young boy home had also been made by Section Commander George Reynolds. So, the arrival of Jimmy Mahon and Frances O'Flaherty was most welcome.

What Malone did not know, however, was that de Valera had the garrison removed from the schoolhouse and assigned to Boland's Mills. By noon, out of the 50 Volunteers which had originally defended the Mount Street Bridge area, there were only 17 left, a handful of Volunteers to defend against two battalions of British soldiers.

Frances O'Flaherty was an early activist in the Irish Republican Brotherhood under Pearse. A former actress, she was also a protester against the conscription of Irish soldiers in the British Army. During the Rising she was tasked initially by Pearse along with other members of the Cumann na mBan with messenger and nursing service. This would change as things heated up.

Her companion, Jimmy Mahon, had no reservations about women as troopers. He himself was a member of the Irish Citizen Army which had Countess Markiewicz and others on active duty. Originally, he served with James Connolly and the ICA in the attack on Dublin Castle. They were repulsed and forced to retreat to the GPO. Now, he would have his revenge.

THE BATTLE OF MOUNT STREET BRIDGE

One would think that the Battle of Mount Street Bridge would be in the annals of military history along with the Charge of the Light Brigade, and that it would be made famous in poetry and song. It had all the elements of the famous Tennyson poem: A blunder by the commander, a headlong assault that was repulsed and ended in the death of many British soldiers.

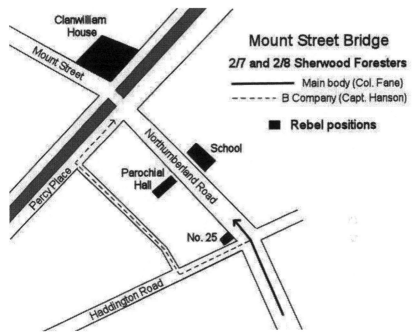

Mount Street Bridge

2/7 and 2/8 Sherwood Foresters

———— Main body (Col. Fane)
– – – – – – B Company (Capt. Hanson)

■ Rebel positions

Clanwilliam House

Mount Street

Northumberland Road

Percy Place

Parochial Hall

School

No. 25

Haddington Road

Map #4. British map showing the positions of the Mount Street Bridge defenders.

Was there a man dismayed?
Not though the soldier knew
Someone had blundered.
Theirs not to make reply,
Theirs not to reason why,
Theirs but to do and die.[62]

The British troops who arrived from the 7th and 8th Battalions, also known as the Sherwood Foresters, were originally intended to go to France. There, they would have engaged in trench warfare, the only type of battle for which they had actually been trained. "Up

---

[62] Alfred Lord Tennyson, "The Charge of the Light Brigade" (1854).

and over the top and straight ahead" would be the strategy which was followed by generals on both sides in the Great War. And so it was with the British commanders this day as their troops approached the reinforced buildings which housed the handful of Irish defenders. Contemptuous of the Irish in the first place, overconfident in their superior numbers in the second, they would order their men to charge straight ahead instead of encircling the defenders' positions.

At around noon the first rebel volleys hit the forward sections of the British troops marching in from Dun Laoghaire. It seemed to some that 25 Northumberland Road, a house at the junction with Haddington Road, was the source of the firing but the number of rebels was unknown. Although there were only two of the original defenders there, Mick Malone and Seamus Grace, they had been joined by Jimmy Mahon and Frances O'Flaherty. Malone was armed with a Mauser machine pistol, while Grace, Mahon, and O'Flaherty had the Lee-Enfields. While the other defenders were mostly armed with the older Howth rifles which emitted black powder and made their locations obvious, the defenders at 25 Northumberland Road gave no such indication. The quiet, largely Loyalist, residential street now echoed with the screams of wounded and dying British soldiers.

If the officers had ordered their men to outflank 25 Northumberland Road and then gone on to Baggot Street to the west, they could have proceeded to St. Stephen's Green and the city center. Instead, two platoons formed a line and attacked the barricaded house. They were driven back by fire from Malone's machine pistol on the third floor and sporadic fire from lower floors by Grace and his ICA allies. They were ordered to regroup and attack again. Again, they were repulsed with several casualties both dead and wounded.

Around 1pm others of the battalion marched over to Percy Place which ran on the south side of the canal between the Mount Street bridge and Baggot Street where they came under fire by the Irish defenders. Now they faced rebel volleys in front and from their left. The fire from the left was apparently snipers near de Valera's command some distance away at Jacob's Mills. It was sporadic and mostly ineffective but distracted the troops from their goal, creating noise, more havoc, and black clouds of smoke. The British troops huddled for cover along the Canal. Their officers ordered another frontal assault which also failed as the rebel force of only 13 men and one woman defended their small bit of turf.

At about 5pm additional reinforcements arrived, along with hand grenades and a Lewis machine gun. Lieutenant Malone, getting low on ammunition and realizing the hopelessness of his position, ordered Mahon and O'Flaherty to vacate the premises and escape so that they might live to fight another day. Shortly thereafter British soldiers were able to get near enough to throw a hand grenade which blew down the front door of 25 Northumberland Street, At the same time as British troops had gained entry through the back door on Percy Street, Seamus Grace, who was standing in the hallway, shouted for Malone and the others to get out while he covered their escape. Unfortunately, his gun jammed, so he wheeled around and headed for the cellar. As Malone came down the stairs firing his machine pistol, the British responded with a volley of bullets, killing him instantly. Intending to finish off Grace and any remaining defenders, the British threw a couple of grenades into the cellar, collapsing part of the ceiling and one wall, then abandoned the building assuming anyone left would be dead.

In an interesting twist of fate, however, Grace survived. He had ducked behind an old iron stove and was able to avoid serious injury. Mahon and O'Flaherty had departed with the first warning by Malone and had disappeared. Flaherty, like several other women, would recover a British Lee-Enfield from a fallen British soldier and use it to great effect against the British in the final days of the Rising.

The British next moved to the schoolhouse which they thought was occupied but was in fact abandoned. Before they arrived, they had to pass the Parochial Hall where, according to British reports, they encountered heavy fire from the rebels. However, given the small number of Volunteers still involved in the combat (only 14 out of the original 17) it is unlikely that it was heavy. It was constant, though, and unnerving especially for British soldiers in their first combat experience. The Howth rifle was powerful and made a devastating wound upon impact. It was also loud and resulted in a cloud of black smoke when fired. These elements, coupled with rapid-fire machine pistols from some of the volunteers, plus the midafternoon heat and the confusion of battle in which "friendly" fire may have played a part, might have given many of the Sherwood Foresters and their leaders the feeling that they were facing a much larger rebel force. Moreover, the rebel fire was highly accurate and within minutes the street lay littered with British dead and wounded.

But the tide was about to change. The defenders in the Parochial Hall were now out of ammunition and totally outnumbered. When they tried to retreat via the back door, they were immediately surrounded by British troops and captured. They were held in custody until their captors received orders as to where they should be taken. One of the guards, irate at the loss of life on the part of his comrades, pushed Volunteer Joe Clark up against the doorway and fired at him. He missed (incredibly, at such short range)[63] and the shot went through the door, narrowly missing a doctor who had come to treat the wounded.

The British troops now moved to Clanwilliam House which was defended by a handful of men, including James Doyle, George Reynolds, Daniel Byrne and William Ronan. At this location they had a perfect view of the British as they advanced up Northumberland Street toward the Mount Street Bridge. This would be the last pitched battle in the area. The defenders opened fire from the windows on all three floors, shooting at will down at the British soldiers. The dead and wounded lay across the road like casualties at Ypres or Verdun, and Volunteer James Doyle and others ordered a

---

[63] This incident, among many other under-reported examples, shows just how poorly trained many of the British soldiers were. The rebels had practiced marksmanship for many months, and that included several women such as Constance Markiewicz and Margaret Skinnider, who were crack sharpshooters. This inept British soldier standing a few feet away from a stationary target missed his mark.

ceasefire after seeing two brave nurses, Florence Williams and Louise Nolan from nearby Sir Patrick Dun's Hospital, risking their lives to treat the wounded. Both women were later to receive medals of bravery from the British Empire. General-in-Chief John Maxwell later praised the "gallant assistance by a number of medical men, ladies, nurses and woman servants who at great risk attended the wounded."[64]

Despite there being alternative routes across the canal nearby, Brigadier General Lowe ordered repeated frontal assaults on the Mount Street position. It would be similar to the strategy employed at the Battle of the Somme three months later although the latter would have far more devastating results.[65] At any rate, having failed in previous onslaughts, around 8pm a squad of British soldiers did finally manage to get over the bridge under cover of machine-gun fire. Unable to get through the barricaded front entrance of Clanwilliam House, they climbed through the window and began throwing grenades into each room in an effort to clear the building. The house soon caught on fire and the last defenders were captured, with the burned corpses recovered days later.

While British and Irish historians differ in their documentation of this famous battle, it is clear that it was a major defeat for the British Army. It had taken nearly nine hours for the British to advance 300 yards with 1,750 troops against 14 rebels. British casualties numbered 234 including 18 officers. The Irish had four killed and eight captured. The captured Volunteers were taken to Ladd Street Barracks, then transported to various prisons in England and Wales.

---

[64] Part of the "great risk" came from the fact the British attempted to use the ceasefire to advance their positions. Therefore, the rebels ended it.

[65] At the Battle of the Somme (July 1-November 18, 1916) with repeated frontal assaults on German positions the British Army advanced a maximum of seven miles. British casualties on the first day numbered 57,000 with 19,240 killed. It was the bloodiest day in British military history.

Fig. 29. Clanwilliam House shortly after its capture by the British after being defended by a mere seven Volunteers during a fierce battle. One can see by the windows the number of excellent vantages the rebel sharpshooters possessed as the British led their headlong assaults.

Fig. 30. Three members of Cumann na mBan with captured Lee-Enfield rifles. Photograph by Delia McDevitt.

While some women speedily gathered up the valuable Lee-Enfield rifles for use in further battles, others tended to the wounded and dying on both sides. Symbolic of the divide, many in Cumann na mBan would later condemn these heroic nurses for giving aid and comfort to the enemy. While Irish nurses treated British soldiers, the soldiers themselves were often not as gracious in return. After the battle, several had their Red Cross armbands stripped from their uniforms and were arrested and accused of being spies. Meanwhile, the good upper-class citizens of the tree-lined Mount Street neighborhood cheered the victory of the imperial army which they considered protectors of their wealthy homes and property. It was clear to many who lived nearby but were of less prosperous means, that the Rising itself would not resolve these differences. The words of James Connolly, suffering from bullet wounds, would soon be forgotten by all but a few. Yet, they were prophetic of the economic discrepancies which would be multiplied many times in the years to come.

If you remove the English army to-morrow and hoist the green flag over Dublin Castle, unless you set about the organisation of the Socialist Republic your efforts would be in vain. That is to say, you must guarantee that when Ireland is free of foreign domination, the green-coated Irish soldiers will guard the fraudulent gains of capitalist and landlord from 'the thin hands of the poor' just as remorselessly and just as effectually as the scarlet-coated emissaries of England do today.[66]

---

[66] Peter Beresford Ellis (ed.), *James Connolly - Selected Writings* (London: Pluto Press, 1988), 124.

20

JAMES CONNOLLY, REVOLUTIONARY AND FEMINIST

Feminism was not a popular movement in conservative Ireland at the time, nor was it in continental Europe or the United States. Many conservative Irish women accepted their assigned roles in society as wives and homemakers as fitting and proper. The Church enforced that view of things. It was a complex situation full of seeming contradictions. Some revolutionary women such as those in the Cumann na mBan condemned the best qualities of their gender, compassion and empathy, when they criticized nurses for coming to the aid of fallen British soldiers.

While most men held to traditional views as well, there were some notable exceptions. James Connolly was one such man. Hanna Sheehy-Skeffington, founder of the Irish Women's Workers League, described him as "the soundest and most thorough going feminist of all the Irish Labour men."[67] As noted earlier, Connolly was the only leader of the rebellion that not only welcomed, but actively recruited women into the Irish Republican Army. Of the 2100 who fought in Dublin, 37 were women who were acknowledged combatants. He also gave orders to his commanders that other women could be given combat roles if they were willing. Michael Mallin, Commandant of the forces at St. Stephen's Green, gave both Countess Markiewicz and Margaret Skinnider multiple combat assignments.

Connolly, who was born in an Irish ghetto called Cowgate in Edinburgh, Scotland, went to work at the age of 11. At 14, he enlisted

[67] Liam Cahill, "Connolly. Just a Name on a Station or a Hospital?", *The Twelve O'Clock Blog,* May 12, 2020 (https://liamcahill.wordpress.com/2020/05/12/connolly-just-a-name-on-a-station-or-hospital/, accessed Jan 24, 2021).

in the British Army to escape the grinding poverty of slum life. He served for seven years and developed a lasting hatred both for the British Empire which had extended its imperialism to two fifths of the planet, and the army which had enforced that rule through a worldwide system of dependencies—colonies, protectorates, and other territories—and the administration of its proxy governments in Ireland, Scotland, Wales, India, Australia, Egypt, parts of the Americas, South Africa, and the Far East.[68]

In his twenties, Connolly became involved in labor politics and was a member of the Industrial Workers of the World (IWW). He was invited to Ireland (the homeland of his parents and central to his identity) where he worked as the secretary of the Irish Socialist Club. He was the founding editor of *The Socialist* newspaper. He travelled to the US and worked on a newspaper there as well as writing articles on labor, human rights, and socialism. There, he published the first of his many books and pamphlets.[69]

In 1910 he returned to Ireland and was quickly absorbed in labor protests. He participated in the Dublin lockout in which over 20,000 workers staged a general strike, which was forcibly put down by Dublin police siding with the owners. At least two people were killed and over 200 seriously wounded from clubbings and gunshots.[70] In response to the bloody police violence, Connolly and James Larkin and others formed the Irish Citizen Army to protect the workers. This was the beginning of the brigade of 200 which would later join the Volunteers as a united force in the Rising.

By 1915 the British had offered Home Rule for Ireland, but Connolly felt that it was a poor bargain, that Britain would also begin conscripting men to fight in World War I against Germany. Asserting that peace could be secured only through the fall of the capitalist states, he committed the Irish labor movement to opposing the

[68] Tomás O'Riordan, *James Connolly. Multitext Project in Irish History* (University College Cork, Ireland).
[69] Carl Reeve and Ann Barton Reeve, *James Connolly and the United States: The Road to the 1916 Irish Rebellion* (Atlantic Highlands, N.J.: Humanities Press, 1978), 10.
[70] This was the first "Bloody Sunday" in Ireland which would be replicated under different circumstances in the Bogside area of Derry, Northern Ireland in 1972.

Allied war effort. The Irish Republican Brotherhood urged him to be practical and to work through the system. But Conolly demurred. In one of his books, he had written:

> Don't be practical in politics. To be practical in that sense means that you have schooled yourself to think along those lines, and in the grooves that those who rob you would like you to think. [71]

He wrote in the *Workers' Republic*:

> The cry for a union of classes is in reality an insidious move on the part of our Irish master class to have the powers of government transferred from the hands of the English capitalist government to the hands of an Irish capitalist government and to pave the way for this change by inducing the Irish worker to abandon all hopes of bettering his own position.[72]

Connolly's militancy had threatened to interfere with the Irish Republican Brotherhood's plans for a much later insurrection, but in January 1916 he reached a cooperative agreement with the Brotherhood and his 200-strong contingent of the Citizen Army joined forces with the Irish Volunteers in a republican army in which he was commandant general. He would have differences of opinion with many in the IRB including Pearse and de Valera. His belief in full equality for women was one of the major differences. Pearse was a middle-class schoolteacher, de Valera a graduate of the Royal University of Dublin and a mathematics professor. Neither were of the working class. Both were intellectuals and Irish speakers very much involved in the Gaelic League promoting a return to traditional values and the native language. Connolly gave a nod to the Gaelic League when he wrote, "The Gaelic League realizes that capitalism

[71] James Connolly, "Socialism Made Easy", 1909, extracted on *Marxists* (https://www.marxists.org/archive/connolly/1909/sme-la/sme2.htm, accessed Jan. 25, 2021).
[72] James Connolly, "The Re-Conquest of Ireland." (1898) from James Connolly: Lost Writngs. (https://www.marxists.org/archive/connolly/1899/09/reconq.htm)

did more in one century to destroy the tongue of the Gael than the sword of the Saxon did in six."[73] But he was distrustful of those who asserted class and male superiority. He felt that only a fellow laborer could feel how the women's cause was the same as theirs.

In his 1915 work, *The Re-Conquest of Ireland,* he wrote:

> In Ireland the women's cause is felt by all Labour men and women as their cause; the Labour cause has no more earnest and whole-heart-ed supporters than the militant women. Rebellion, even in thought, produces a mental atmosphere of its own; the mental atmosphere the women's rebellion produced, opened their eyes and trained their minds to an understanding of the effects upon their sex of a social system in which the weakest must inevitably go to the wall, and when a further study of the capitalist system taught them that the term 'the weakest' means in practice the most scrupulous, the gentlest, the most humane, the most loving and compassionate, the most honourable, and the most sympathetic, then the militant women could not fail to see, that capi-talism penalised in human beings just those characteristics of which women supposed themselves to be the most complete embodiment.[74]

Although he was a warrior and the actual combat leader of the Rising, he was not disposed to criticize those women who acted out of compassion and helped treat the English soldiers after they had fallen. He realized that what was missing from the masculine-dominated society was precisely those qualities that tempered the brutality of human conflict.

Connolly did not consider that female employment, which many American women would clamor for later in the century, was a solution to the equality problem. He envisioned instead what we have in fact witnessed in the late twentieth and early twenty-first century: Immigrant women being forced into domestic labor to support

[73] *Ibid.*
[74] James Connolly, *The Re-Conquest of Ireland*, Chapter Six, 1915, *Marxists.org* (https://www.marxists.org/archive/connolly/1915/rcoi/chap06.htm, accessed Mar. 4, 2021).

themselves and their families, or working in *maquiladoras*, low-paid factories turning out tennis shoes and clothing for sales in boutiques and outlets in more prosperous lands. In his time, it was Irish women who emigrated to the US, England, and other industrialized nations to labor for slave wages. In the present time, it is Hondurans, Filipinos, Haitians, and Bangladeshi who fill the ranks left by Bridget and Molly. As Connolly notes:

> Just as the present system in Ireland has made cheap slaves or untrained emigrants of the flower of our peasant women, so it has darkened the lives and starved the intellect of the female operatives in mills, shops and factories. Wherever there is a great demand for female labour, as in Belfast, we find that the woman tends to become the chief support of the house. Driven out to work at the earliest possible age, she remains fettered to her wage-earning – a slave for life. Marriage does not mean for her a rest from outside labour, it usually means that, to the outside labour, she has added the duty of a double domestic toil. Throughout her life she remains a wage-earner; completing each day's work, she becomes the slave of the domestic needs of her family; and when at night she drops wearied upon her bed, it is with the knowledge that at the earliest morn she must find her way again into the service of the capitalist, and at the end of that coming day's service for him hasten homeward again for another round of domestic drudgery. So her whole life runs – a dreary pilgrimage from one drudgery to another; the coming of children but serving as milestones in her journey to signalise fresh increases to her burdens. Overworked, underpaid, and scantily nourished because underpaid, she falls easy prey to all the diseases that infect the badly-constructed 'warrens of the poor'. Her life is darkened from the outset by poverty, and the drudgery to which poverty is born, and the starvation of the intellect follows as an inevitable result upon the too early drudgery of the body.[75]

[75] Ibid.

The solution had to be an equality which provided free education to all Irish citizens, both men and women. The "starvation of the intellect" which occurred when women were forced to work at menial jobs to support their families, robbed the country of one of its most valuable resources: intelligent, educated women. A country deprived of the intellectual contribution of half its population could not progress or produce a decent quality of life. Long before Virginia Woolf wrote *A Room of One's Own*, Connolly foresaw that even if a woman had a decent job, paying a fair wage, she would still be at a disadvantage in society in which "women's work" continued to be her sole responsibility in the home at the end of the. A dominant culture which espoused that domestic vision could never result in a liberated society even if the Rising were successful. What was required was a true revolution, not merely a release from the chains of British imperialism; not only the demise of an exploitive laissez faire capitalism and the rise of a social welfare state, but a cultural and moral transformation into a society which regarded all of its members as true citizens sharing the same rights and opportunities, and the same responsibilities. It was why he actively recruited women in the Irish Citizen Army. He hoped that, after sharing the same obligations and risks as their male counterparts, they would be respected at the end and granted the long-overdue rights and opportunities that the men had. And it was why he persuaded Pearse to include "every Irishman and Irishwoman" in the Proclamation of Easter Monday. For as he so compellingly argued:

> Of what use to such sufferers can be the re-establishment of any form of Irish State if it does not embody the emancipation of womanhood. As we have shown, the whole spirit and practice of modern Ireland, as it expresses itself through its pastors and masters, bear socially and politically, hardly upon women. That spirit and that practice had their origins in the establishment in this country of a social and political order based upon the private ownership of property, as against the older order based upon the common ownership of a related community...

None so fitted to break the chains as they who wear them, none so well equipped to decide what is a fetter. In its march towards freedom, the working class of Ireland must cheer on the efforts of those women who, feeling on their souls and bodies the fetters of the ages, have arisen to strike them off, and cheer all the louder if in its hatred of thraldom and passion for freedom the women's army forges ahead of the militant army of Labour.[76]

Fig. 31. James Connolly monument in Chicago's Union Park,
erected by the Irish-American Labor Council of Chicago in October 2008
(photograph by James Curry).

---

[76]   Ibid.

DAY FOUR - THURSDAY, APRIL 27

At the end of Day three, de Valera and his 100 men were still safe in Jacob's Factory and had not come to the aid of the outnumbered fighters defending the Mount Street Bridge area. De Valera had given several conflicting orders during the day but beyond some sporadic sniping from that position, no significant aid was forthcoming. General Lowe next ordered a company of men to work throughout the night digging slit trenches in the field behind the South Dublin Union, which enabled troops to fire on the Marrowbone Lane Distillery in the morning of April 27. However, their fire was mostly ineffective.

What began to be more successful, however, was their heavy fire from both machine guns and artillery at the GPO and the Four Courts area. They also attacked North King Street and the South Dublin Union. They captured Capel Street Bridge and overran several blockades, but nevertheless the GPO still held out. The loss of Capel Street, however, left British troops in a position to blockade any assistance from Volunteers in the Four Courts area communicating with or helping those in the GPO.

While Pearse may have been the titular Commander-in-Chief, Connolly had been in charge of the military operations. He was fearless, venturing out into the streets to direct his men. On one of these sorties, he suffered a bullet wound to his left shoulder and received aid from a medic without attracting any attention to his injury. He continued to fight, and on one of his sorties to Liffey Street near the Ha'penny Bridge, he was seriously wounded in the left ankle leaving him unable to walk. He was carried back to the GPO where he was treated by a captured British doctor. However, the injury was serious, and he would spend the rest of the week on a propped-up mattress with the wound becoming gangrenous due to lack of antibiotics. Nevertheless, he would continue to command and even assist in the evacuation of the GPO when that became necessary.

By the end of the day, major businesses on Sackville Street had suffered heavy damage due to the bombardment from the British gunboat *Helga* on the Liffey River. The oil works had exploded, and the rebels were forced to retreat from O'Connell Bridge and their barricades along Henry Street to the relative safety of the GPO headquarters. One would say "relative safety," because by now fires had broken out on the roof due to incendiary shells fired by the British. Moreover, the heat and sparks from the burning *Times* warehouse had caused fires that the rebels were barely able to control even when the wind died down. They were fired upon by machine guns throughout the night and more incendiary devices were planted and shells fired by the British as dawn approached. Across the street Clery's and the Imperial Hotel burned unattended and molten glass poured into the street.

21
ELIZABETH O'FARRELL AND WINNIFRED CARNEY: PRELUDE TO SURRENDER

Elizabeth O'Farrell was educated by the Sisters of Mercy but when her father died, she was forced to forgo further training as a nurse and midwife to go to work. She took a job at Armstrong's Printers in Dublin, her father's former employer. In 1914 she joined the Cumann na mBan and supported the early work of the Irish Volunteers as a messenger.

During the Rising she performed many tasks, including delivering dispatches from the GPO to the other locations throughout the city. She also carried food and ammunition to rebel outposts, hiding the contraband under her full skirts. In the first days of the Rising, she bicycled from the GPO to St Stephen's Green, Boland's Mills, Jacob's Factory and Four Courts performing this service. However, with the wounding of James Connolly and others she began assisting her best friend Nurse Julia Grenan in treating the casualties at the GPO.

On Friday, April 28 the Volunteers and Irish Citizen Army fighters at the Post Office were low on food, medicine, and ammunition. Covered with dust and rubble, with no clean water or bandages, they decided to evacuate the women and the wounded. When they had accomplished that feat during intermittent shelling from British heavy artillery, O'Farrell stayed behind. She was joined by her friend Nurse Grenan, and by Winnifred Carney who had been in the GPO from the beginning.

Carney, a Belfast socialist, feminist and republican, was educated at the Christian Brothers School on Donegall Street in that city and taught school there for a while after her graduation. Looking for a higher salary, she decided to train as a secretary and get a credential as a shorthand typist, a skill restricted to men at that time and used primarily by court reporters and barristers' assistants. When she graduated from the Hughes Commercial Academy, she was among the first women in Ireland to be so qualified.

Fig. 32. Winnifred Carey, ca. 1912.

In 1912 she met James Connolly while he was organizing unions in Belfast. The two immediately hit it off and formed a partnership which would last throughout Connolly's lifetime. She joined him in his unionizing efforts and was especially active in getting women in the garment industry unionized. In a moving manifesto which was published and widely distributed she described the Belfast mills as "slaughterhouses and penitentiaries for children."[77] She urged the women in the mills to unite and fight for better conditions.

[77] "Winifred Carney: Belfast socialist, feminist and republican", *Culture Northern Ireland* (https://www.culturenorthernireland.org/article/637/winifred-carney) Accessed Mar. 4, 2021.)

Ultimately her efforts bore fruit and she became secretary of the Textile Union.

She also became active in the Gaelic League with the mission to revitalize Irish language and culture and made efforts to see that these subjects were taught in the Belfast schools. In addition, she was a leader in the suffragette movement to get women the right to vote. During the Dublin lockout she raised funds to support those workers who had come to Belfast after losing their jobs. She was part of the anti-conscription movement to help more young men resist the British Army's push in the summer of 1914 to obtain Irish recruits for the "War to End All Wars".

That same year she joined the Irish Citizen Army and Cumann na mBan and became active in discussions and in planning for the future of the organizations. In 1915 she met with various members of both groups and was privy to Connolly's plans for the Rising. A week before Easter 1916, Connolly telegraphed her to come to London to be by his side.

She met with Connolly who asked her to become his aide-de-camp and official secretary. She agreed. She began working assiduously at Liberty Hall preparing confidential correspondence for Connolly with the newly united force integrating Cumann na mBan, the Irish Volunteers and the ICA into the "Army of the Irish Republic."

When the Rising broke out on Easter Monday, April 24, she strapped on a Webley pistol and joined Connolly at Liberty Hall where, in his role as Commandant-General of the United Forces in Dublin, he gave out the various assignments to the division commandants. She would be by his side for the remainder of the week: typing dispatches, giving instructions to couriers, and organizing the relaying of reports. After he was shot, she would be by his side as a nurse. She would not only be the last of the women, along with Elizabeth O'Farrell and Julia Granen, to leave the GPO when it caught on fire from British artillery; she would also be the one who would meticulously type out the final surrender orders from Pearse which would be distributed by O'Farrell to the various outposts.[78]

DAY FIVE - FRIDAY, APRIL 28

BRITISH ASSAULTS INCREASE, AS DO THEIR LOSSES

In the area of St. Stephen's Green and the College of Surgeons there were now major shortages of food and water. British snipers took aim at couriers trying to bring relief and the effort had to be abandoned. Outside the GPO the British continued their artillery barrage and machine-gun attacks, as well as launching incendiary grenades, destroying a large part of the classical edifice. Attempts to put out the fires proved futile. In addition, the British set up barricades on Moore Street to enfilade rebel positions.

In the Four Courts area and on North King Street things were more hopeful. The rebels at Four Courts had more ammunition at this point than when the Rising began. In addition, they had more captured British weapons. Commandant Ned Daly at North King Street had provided formidable defensive barricades. A foolish frontal attack on one of his positions left 14 dead and 32 wounded from the South Staffordshire regiment. Noted one rebel years later, "To this day, I can't understand why they tried to rush things." [79]

When the British commander Colonel Taylor attempted to remedy the situation by sending an armored truck with more reinforcements, the Volunteers picked them off one by one. The resistance continued well into the next day and provoked a retaliation by the British soldiers which would result in the wholesale slaughter of civilians, and the murder of captured prisoners.

General Lowe later noted:

[78] (https://www.bbc.co.uk/programmes/articles/19ytB8NQdgzxg95sDMdDhb2/winifred-carney) Accessed March 4, 2021.
[79] Townshend, *op. cit.*, 293.

The casualties were very heavy during the fighting. The troops were continually fired at from the roofs and upper windows of the houses. With modern rifles it is impossible to tell by the sound from which direction a shot has come. The rebels were moving from house to house. As the troops for instance moved along the street the rebels would escape out back doors and fire again at the troops from practically every house.[80]

The mention of "modern weapons" clearly shows the use of captured British Lee-Enfields rather than the Howth 1876 Mausers with which the Volunteers were originally armed when the attack began. Nevertheless, the remark was both misleading and self-serving. It was misleading because the bulk of British casualties came when they attacked fortified barricades, so they clearly knew "from which direction a shot ha[d] come." It was self-serving because the general did not offer this excuse until an investigation into the civilian deaths was ordered by the high command, and he clearly wanted to exculpate the officers involved in the intentional murder of civilians.

ABANDONING THE GPO HEADQUARTERS

Meanwhile, shelling increased, the GPO itself caught fire and began to burn out of control. Ernie O'Malley, a medical student, watched from the northside of the building, "The fire had spread, it seemed as if the whole centre of the city was in flames. Sparks shot up and the fire jumped high as the wind increased." [81]

Pearse ordered everyone remaining in the GPO to evacuate. A sortie led by Michael O'Rahilly led the way but was badly shot up – 21 out of 30 men were hit by fire from the ever-closer British guns.

---

[80] Statement of General John Maxwell, quoted in John Dorney, "The North King Street Massacre, Dublin 1916", *The Irish Story*, Apr. 13, 2012 (https://www.theirishstory.com/2012/04/13/the-north-king-street-massacre-dublin-1916/#.YKANA6hKgdU, accessed Mar. 10, 2021.)

[81] Ernie O'Malley (author) and Corman O'Malley (editor), *On Another Man's Wound: Ernie O'Malley and Ireland's War for Independence* (Dublin: Mercier Press, 2013), 46.

O'Rahilly himself was killed and lay sprawled, face up, on Henry Street in full view of his comrades. The survivors, led by Pearse and Plunkett, escaped the blazing Post Office onto the little streets around Moore Street. There the three women and the remaining Volunteers tunneled through walls, to occupy the terrace location on numbers 10 to 25 Moore Street

Once they were temporarily secure in their new location, they assessed the situation. They knew it was only a matter of time before the British began shelling the buildings on Moore Streets with their heavy artillery. After some discussion that evening among the leaders of the Provisional Government it became apparent that they were hopelessly outnumbered and outgunned with the British forces now consisting of over 6,000 men, plus a gunboat on the river, several machine guns, and heavy artillery. In addition, they were low on ammunition and could not continue even a perfunctory attempt at battle. It was decided that they would approach the British command to negotiate a surrender to prevent further loss of life.

DAY SIX - SATURDAY, APRIL 29

On Saturday 29, Pearse met with Elizabeth O'Farrell and asked her if she would be willing to go to approach the British lines and request a meeting on his behalf with the General-in-Chief of the British forces to discuss the terms of a ceasefire. O'Farrell agreed to volunteer for this assignment. At 12:45, wearing a Red Cross armband and carrying a white flag of truce, she approached the British blockade at the intersection of Moore and Parnell Streets. The message she was to pass on was that the Commandant-General of the Irish Republican Army would like to treat with the head of the British forces in Ireland. That would have been General John Maxwell.

The British sentries on duty, however, were not quite sure what to do with her. She was obviously not in the uniform of the Irish Citizen Army, nor did she represent herself as an officer of any group. She was a civilian and, as far as they could determine, a non-combatant. Did she truly have any authorization to see the general or was she just a woman acting on her own initiative to end the conflict? In the latter case, of course, she could be safely ignored. Unwilling to contact headquarters and disturb General Maxwell, they sent a message to Brigadier General William Lowe who was in command of the forces at Trinity College. Meanwhile, O'Farrell was detained by the soldiers in Tom Clarke's shop at the corner of Parnell and upper Sackville Streets.

General Lowe, upon receiving the message, set out from Trinity College with his son, a young lieutenant, and his staff officer Captain Courcy-Wheeler. Lowe met with Elizabeth at 1.30pm at Clarke's shop and told her that he would not treat with Pearce on terms or conditions. He said that Pearse must surrender unconditionally. She was then escorted back to the barricade and made her way back to the rebel positions on Moore Street. Pearse gave her another note in which he specified his conditions for surrender. Again, O'Farrell went back to the barricade. There, Lowe reiterated his statement that he would accept no conditions.

The remaining Volunteers and ICA fighters had a discussion at 16 Moore Street in which it was proposed that they try to break out once more. Some of the younger Volunteers and Citizen Army men wanted to make a last stand on Moore Street. One of the most vocal was the new field commander, 20-year-old Sean McLaughlin, appointed to replace Connolly who was indisposed because of his wounds. Others suggested that they could try to get to the Four Courts area and connect with Daly's men. Séan MacDermott, speaking for the organizers of the Rising, argued that they had done all that could be expected of them. They had in fact made the blood sacrifice which he had once said would be necessary for the free republic to be born. Indeed, his execution, which he foretold, would in fact be a part of that sacrifice.[82] The elders prevailed.

---

[82] As an elder (he was 33) and a leader in the IRB, he said that the only deaths which would follow a surrender would be those of the leaders such as himself. He argued that the younger men should stand down so that they could return to fight another day.

With O'Rahilly dead, and one of Connolly's two bullet wounds turned gangrenous, their patio on Moore Street surrounded by British rifles and machine guns and a heavy artillery piece primed to fire into the front of the building, further resistance was hopeless. To make matters worse, three elderly civilians who lived in one of the Moore Street residences and tried to escape were cut down by British machine guns while Pearse looked helplessly on.

After witnessing that slaughter, Pearse decided that he would reply to Lowe's request. He sent a terse note with Elizabeth O'Farrell, stating he wished to surrender to "prevent the further slaughter of the civilian population and in the hope of saving our followers, now hopelessly surrounded and outnumbered."[83]

After delivering the final message and having it accepted, she was once again returned. Pearse emerged from the Moore Street house and the two walked side by side back to the barricade. In the words of Captain Courcy-Wheeler:

> At 2.30 pm Commandant-General Pearse surrendered to General Lowe accompanied by myself and Lieutenant Lowe at the junction of Moore Street and Great Britain Street. He handed over his arms and military equipment. His sword and automatic repeating pistol in a holster with a pouch of ammunition, and his canteen (sic), which contained two large onions, were handed to me by Commandant-General Pearse.[84]

O'Farrell and many others were not in agreement with Pearse's decision. There were still rebel strongholds that were formidable. De Valera's position was still strong, for example, as was MacDonagh's at Jacob's Factory, Daly's at Four Courts, and Ceannt's at South Dublin Union.

---

[83] Townshend, *op. cit.*, 246.
[84] In British English the word canteen refers to mess kit, not just the flask for liquids. Thus, the two large onions are not so incongruous.

22

AIRBRUSHED FROM HISTORY?

The photo of Pearse standing in front of Lieutenant John Lowe (l) and Brigadier General William Lowe was taken at the corner of Parnell and Moore Streets by an amateur photographer using a box camera. He gave the negative to John Cashman and the photo was subsequently published on the front page of the *London Daily Sketch* (May 10, 1916) with some alterations.

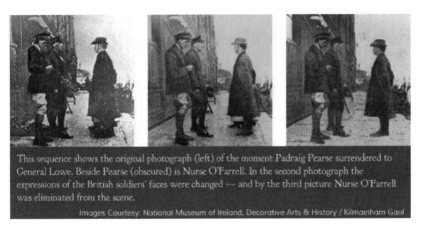

This sequence shows the original photograph (left) of the moment Padraig Pearse surrendered to General Lowe. Beside Pearse (obscured) is Nurse O'Farrell. In the second photograph the expressions of the British soldiers' faces were changed — and by the third picture Nurse O'Farrell was eliminated from the scene.

Images Courtesy: National Museum of Ireland, Decorative Arts & History / Kilmainham Gaol

Fig. 33. Commandant Pearse, accompanied by Nurse O'Farrell, surrenders to General Lowe.

As we can observe in the original, the skirt and shoes of O'Farrell are clearly seen. However, in subsequent versions of the photograph, both the feet and the edge of the skirt disappear. It has been suggested by many authors that the evidence of O'Farrell's presence had been airbrushed from history.[85]

More recent research by Michael Barry, author of *Courage Boys, We Are Winning*, a photographic history of the Easter Rising, makes a strong case that no such airbrushing took place. First, by her own admission, O'Farrell apparently chose not to be in the photo.

> Miss O'Farrell and her great friend Miss Julia Grenan spent a few days with us in May 1956. If you examine the photograph of Pearse surrendering to General Lowe, you will notice the shoe and dress of a nurse on the far side of Pearse. She told us that when she saw a British soldier getting ready to take the photo, she stepped back beside Pearse so as not to give the enemy press any satisfaction. Ever after she regretted having done so.[86]

Furthermore, according to Barry, airbrushing was a much later technique. What likely occurred was that the original image taken from the negative was simply cleaned up. It was a very poor-quality amateur photo. A technician at the paper simply painted out the shoes and skirt edge and painted in Lowe's puttees and sharpened the paving stones. Barry concluded quite convincingly that there was no underlying gender prejudice or political agenda for the removal of the bit of skirt or shoes.[87]

After meeting with General Lowe, Pearse was then taken to General John Maxwell, the newly arrived British commander, to confirm the unconditional surrender in person.

---

[85] Mary Thorpe, "Elizabeth O'Farrell: Nurse and Rebel – Airbrushed from Irish History", *The Wild Geese*, Jul. 30, 2015 (https://thewildgeese.irish/profiles/blogs/elizabeth-o-farrell-nurse-cumann-na-mban-rebel-and-the-woman-that, accessed Mar. 15, 2021.)

[86] *An Fiolar*, Golden Jubilee Issue (Mount St. Joseph College: Roscrea, 1958), n/p.

[87] Michael Barry, "Airbrushed out of history? Elizabeth O'Farrell and Patrick Pearse's surrender, 1916", March 10, 2016 on *The Irish Story* (https://www.theirishstory.com/2016/03/10/airbrushed-out-of-history-elizabeth-ofarrell-and-patrick-pearses-surrender-1916/#.YF91FK9KgdW, accessed Mar. 15, 2021.)

23

A RELUCTANT SURRENDER

Pearse's surrender of his contingent, including the stretcher-bound Connolly, had no effect on the rest of the rebels' positions which continued to exchange gunfire with the British forces around the city. The garrisons at Jacob's factory, the Four Courts, and the South Dublin Union and the Marrowbone (Jameson) Distillery were still fighting with some success. The British shelling of Boland's Mills was ineffective and resistance there was equally tenacious.

So, Lowe next asked Pearse to write out a surrender order for the outlying rebels and to give him a list of all the positions still armed and fighting. He also suggested that he might "detain Nurse O'Farrell for the night"[88] so that she would be available to take around surrender orders the next day. He promised at the same time to set her free after she accomplished this mission. Pearse asked O'Farrell if she was willing, and she agreed. Pearse was then taken away to write out the final command to his troops in the field:

> In order to prevent further slaughter of the civilian population and in the hope of saving the lives of our followers, the members of the Provisional Government present at Headquarters have decided on an unconditional surrender, and Commandants or Officers commanding

---

[88] "Miss Elizabeth O'Farrell's Story of the Surrender", 1916 Rebellion Museum website (http://1916rebellionmuseum.com/1916-easter-rising/elizabeth-ofarrell/, accessed Mar. 16, 2021.)

districts will order their commands to lay down arms. P.H. Pearse, Dublin, 30th April 1916.[89]

At about 4.15pm. General Lowe returned with Pearse's written order for the other commandants to surrender, and five or six typewritten copies; one of these was signed by James Connolly for his own men in the GPO area and in St. Stephen's Green. General Lowe first gave an order to take to Moore Street, where the Republican troops from the GPO had taken over, and a written note as to how they should surrender. The note read:

> Carrying a white flag, proceed down Moore Street, turn into Moore Lane and Henry Place, out into Henry Street, and around the Pillar to the right-hand side of Sackville Street, march up to within a hundred yards of the military drawn up at the Parnell Statue, halt, advance five paces and lay down arms.[90]

After completing the first leg of her mission, O'Farrell began on the second and, carrying a small white flag and accompanied by a British guard, she headed for the Four Courts. On the way they met with a local priest who offered to accompany them and carry the white flag himself. When they arrived, she gave Commandant Daly the orders from Pearse and told him of the surrender of the Headquarters contingent the previous day. She observed that Daly was strongly entrenched in his position. Quite naturally, O'Farrell remembered, he was very reluctant to surrender. However, he "accepted his orders as a soldier should."[91] She then returned to the British lines and remained under guard that evening.

---

[89] Pádraic Pearse, Handwritten surrender order to all commandants, April 30, 1916. Quoted in "Easter Rising surrender letter handwritten by Pádraig Pearse to fetch over €1million at auction", *The Irish Post*, Dec. 5, 2016 (https://www.irishpost.com/news/easter-rising-surrender-letter-handwritten-by-padraig-pearse-to-fetch-over-€1million-at-auction-but-may-go-to-a-foreign-buyer-108078, accessed Mar. 16, 2021.)

[90] See note 88.

[91] O'Farrell statement. See note 76.

When she stepped out the next morning, she saw the Volunteers who had surrendered per Connolly's and Pearse's order. She estimated that there were between 300-400 men and women including Julia Grenan and Winnifred Carney who were gathered on a small plot of grass in front of the hospital on Great Britain Street with their confiscated packs and weapons at the foot of the statue of Parnell. They had been out there without blankets or food all night shivering in the cold and damp under armed guard. It offended her sense of common humanity to see them thus and hardened her heart against the British for the unnecessary cruelty.

Accompanied by Captain Courcy-Wheeler, she was driven to St. Stephen's Green. While the officer waited in the car, O'Farrell proceeded across the Green with some trepidation since machine-gun fire was still coming from the Shelbourne Hotel as well as answering rifle fire from the College of Surgeons and from various street barricades. Little attention was paid to her small white flag which perhaps was not even seen by some of the combatants.

It was obvious to her that the British captain observing from the street in his official car considered her to be expendable and was unwilling to risk his own by dismounting and offering her an escort. When she arrived at the entrance to the College of Surgeons and stated her mission, she was told that Commandant Mallin was not available, and that Countess Markiewicz was next in command. She gave the Countess the surrender order and told her about the capitulation of the GPO and the Headquarters battalion. Markiewicz, clearly unhappy with this news, took the written order and said that she would discuss it with Commandant Mallin.

When she returned through the hail of fire across the park to the car parked in the street, she found a frosty reception from the British captain who was upset and said that she should have stayed until she received a formal acceptance by Mallin![92]

---

[92] Ironically, this martinet was also married to a cousin of Countess Markiewicz. He would also be the person who would formally accept her surrender and see her sentenced to death.

Next, they headed for Boland's Mills to pass the surrender order to Commandant de Valera. Once again, the captain was reluctant to go to the Mill itself since there were barricades on the way. He stopped the car and instructed her to get out and take the orders the rest of the way on foot.

Once again, she encountered fire from both sides as she made her way through back street to de Valera's headquarters. When she finally arrived safely and gave him the order as well as informing him of the surrender of Pearse and Connolly and the Headquarters battalion, de Valera refused to accept it. He said he could not honor an order from a prisoner, and she would have to consult with his now acting commander, MacDonagh. With the patience and forbearance of Job and the courage of a lion, Elizabeth O'Farrell went out through the perilous streets again. She describes the meeting with MacDonagh and her ultimate success.

At 15 Peter Street I knocked and asked to see Commandant MacDonagh. I was blindfolded and walked for about five minutes. I then heard Commandant MacDonagh's voice and the bandage was taken off my eyes. I gave him the orders from Commandant Pearse and told him of our position in the G.P.O. and Moore Street. He brought me into a small room and told me he would not take orders from a prisoner, that he, himself, was next in command and he would have nothing to say to the surrender until he would confer with General Lowe, the members of the Provisional Government already prisoners, and the officers under his command. An interview was then arranged by Fr. Augustine for Commandant MacDonagh with General Lowe. This took place outside St. Patrick's Park at about 3 o'clock. Commandant MacDonagh then went to Marrowbone Distillery to consult Commandant Ceannt, and after this consultation agreed to surrender also. I remained in Jacob's while all this was taking place, and when Commandant MacDonagh returned, he called the officers together and afterwards told the men there that they had decided to carry out Commandant Pearse's orders. The men were against surrendering, but I heard Commandant MacDonagh say to them: "Boys, it is not my wish to surrender, but after consultation with Commandant Ceannt and other officers, we think it is the best thing to do – if we don't surrender now they will show no mercy to the leaders already prisoners." I then walked down to Bride Street, where Commandant MacDonagh and his men were to surrender. As I waited at the corner of Bride Street, and Ross Road, Commandant MacDonagh came down to the military to complain that a British soldier had entered Jacob's and was firing on his men. An officer was sent back with him and the soldier was placed under arrest. Commandant Ceannt came down the Ross Road at about 6 o'clock p.m. and surrendered with his men and also with the members of the Cumann na mBan who were attached to his command. Both sections of Volunteers were then disarmed, after which Captain Wheeler came over and took me away to the car.[93]

The 22 women at the Marrowbone Distillery were told that they were free to go since they were not active combatants. However, led by Rose Pat McNamara, they declined to leave the men and lined up alongside them. Together the Volunteers and the Cumann na mBan marched off singing a patriotic song.[94] Elizabeth O'Farrell's account concludes:

By this time, it was getting dusk and he [Captain Wheeler] drove to Trinity College to telephone General Lowe to know if it was too late to go back down to Boland's to Commandant de Valera with the orders from Commandant Pearse, which Commandant MacDonagh had countersigned. Whatever information Caption Wheeler received, he conveyed me up to Dublin Castle. It appears that in the meantime de Valera had surrendered.[95]

[93] O'Farrell Statement. See note 76.
[94] Some rebel commanders, like Joe McGrath at Marrowbone Lane, told their men to escape and did so themselves. Michael Mallin, the Citizen Army commander, told anyone who thought they could escape to do so, as did John MacBride in Jacob's factory, adding, if they ever got the chance to fight again, "don't get inside four walls." See Townshend, op.cit., 250-251.
[95] O'Farrell Statement, cited in note 80.

In fact, de Valera had followed Pearse's order after MacDonagh had countersigned it. He and all of his men presented themselves to the British command and laid down their arms, thus effectively ending the Rising.

There were 485 known deaths, 260 of which were civilians. The UK forces lost 126 soldiers, the Irish 82, and 17 policemen were also killed. Forty per cent of those killed were children under the age of 17. Most of the civilian casualties were caused by British machine-gun fire and incendiary shells fired into private homes. Some deaths, such as those during the North King Street massacre, were motivated by a mixture of frustration and revenge. Others, such as those of Francis Sheehy-Skeffington and the two journalists, were clearly murder under the guise of military action.

24
SURRENDER OF FORCES
OUTSIDE OF DUBLIN

W hen Eoin MacNeill issued his order countermanding the
Rising, it was relayed to all Volunteer and ICA officers, and
it was printed in the Sunday morning newspapers. But the Military
Council met at Liberty Hall and decided to go ahead anyway—just
a day later. However, MacNeill's order greatly reduced the number
of Volunteers who would be actively engaged—especially outside
Dublin. To counter this defect in operations, Peace had messages
sent to all the outlying districts and counties. Unfortunately, not
all of them were received or credited, and others arrived too late
to provide either sufficient reinforcements to the Dublin forces,
or timely diversionary action to engage British forces outside of
the city.

COUNTY GALWAY

William Mellows, Commander of the Western Division of Volunteers, received word late Monday evening of the Rising. He mobilized approximately 700 volunteers armed mostly with shotguns
and pistols (some only with pikes) and attacked the Royal Constabulary Barracks. His goal was to divert British forces from Dublin
and tie them up in Galway. After an unsuccessful effort to take that
objective, he moved his troops on to Athenry.

One Volunteer, Michael Newell, describes a brief battle between
the rebels and the RIC.

The enemy advanced on foot on our position, firing all the time. Captain Molloy ordered us to open fire, which we did, but the enemy fire was so intense and the bullets striking the top of the walls, we were compelled to keep down, and we were only able to take an occasional shot.... The enemy then made an attempt to outflank our position but were beaten back. The enemy then retreated and continued to fire until well out of range of our shotguns. [96]

By Thursday, Volunteers realized they could only offer token resistance but decided to continue fighting. Although poorly armed and at a great disadvantage, his troops nevertheless accomplished their goal. The British had to dispatch a warship, the HMS *Gloucester*, to counter the Volunteers' military activities. In addition, they landed 200 marines and shelled the countryside as the rebels retreated using diversionary tactics.

By Friday, almost 1,000 additional British troops were pouring into County Galway. The rebels planned a retreat to Clare just as news was coming through that heavy artillery was being used on Irish positions in Dublin. It was finally decided that, in the face of such overwhelming odds, the force would disband, and the leaders would escape if given the opportunity.

By Saturday, outnumbered and scattered, many were captured while others escaped. Over 300 were eventually deported to prisons in England and Scotland. Mellows escaped to the US, where he was arrested and detained without trial in the Tombs Prison in New York, on a trumped-up charge of attempting to aid Germany in World War I.

COUNTY MEATH

Schoolteacher Thomas Ashe and his Fingal Volunteers, after having been told to stand down by a messenger from MacNeill on Sunday,

---

[96] Mark Maloney, "The 1916 Rising Outside Dublin," *An Phoblacht,* Issue No. 4, 2020 (https://www.anphoblacht.com/contents/27792, accessed Mar. 20, 2021).

were ordered by Pearse on Monday morning to send part of their forces to Dublin and use the remainder to strike the RIC barracks and create diversions outside the city beginning at 1pm. Working with only 45 men and 15 women[97] from the Cumann na mBan, the Fingal Volunteers damaged railway lines, cut telegraph wires and fought using hit-and-run tactics with great success. The largest single engagement was the Battle of Ashbourne in County Meath on Friday. Thirty of Ashe's Volunteers had successfully attacked an RIC barracks and there was a heavy exchange of gunfire on both sides. Finally, after blowing open the doors of the barracks with a grenade, they compelled the RIC to surrender. Before the surrender could be consummated, however, the defenders were relieved with 60 reinforcements. Now outnumbered by more than 3 to 1, the Volunteers were disheartened but under Ashe's firm command settled in for a four-hour battle which resulted in losses on both sides and in the eventual surrender of the barracks. Ashe had the RIC men turn over their weapons and make a solemn promise not to engage in any more activities against the Irish Republic. After they agreed, he released them all with a caution.

They made camp that evening on the outskirts of Dublin and were informed on Saturday of Pearse's general order to surrender.

COUNTY WEXFORD

Volunteer officer Paul Galligan traveled 200 kilometers by bicycle from Dublin with orders from Pádraic Pearse to mobilize. Approximately 200 Volunteers and 70 Cumann na mBan women from the

---

[97] Eight women of the Cumann na mBan gathered at Rath Cross, Ashbourne in 1966 at the fiftieth anniversary of the Battle of Ashbourne. They were Mrs M. Kelly, and Mrs. Anne Grimley, Skerries; Miss Mairead Duke, Miss J. Duke, Miss A. Walsh and Mrs M. O'Connor, St.Margarets and Miss K. Lalloway and Miss K. Prendergast, Navan. "1916 Remembered," *Fingal Independent*, Febr. 25, 2000 (https://www.independent.ie/regionals/fingalindependent/localnotes/1916-remembered-27782911.html, accessed Oct. 9, 2021).

Enniscorthy and Ferns companies assembled ready for combat, commanded by Robert Brennan, Seamus Doyle and Sean Etchingham.

On Thursday of Easter Week, Úna Brennan, Marion Stokes and Greta Comerford raised the tricolor flag over Enniscorthy's Athenaeum Theatre proclaiming the Irish Republic. Out of the more than 70 women present, two of these would later come to the attention of British authorities as prominent participants: Nell Ryan and Kathleen Browne would be singled out for harsh punishment.

Commandants Brennan and Doyle established the rebel headquarters in the Athenaeum. They attacked the RIC barracks, and a gun battle took place in which a RIC officer was wounded. While they could have continued shooting and killing the defenders, a decision was made not to storm the barracks but to force them to surrender in order to capture their arms and ammunition which were urgently needed. By Saturday over 1,000 Volunteers had been mobilized and a detachment was sent to occupy the village of Ferns. They also took over Vinegar Hill, the site of the famous last stand of the United Irishmen in the 1798 rebellion. [98]

Meanwhile the British sent over 1,000 troops to counter them, along with two field artillery pieces and a 4.7 naval gun on an armored train The men and women of County Wexford were not intimidated. Confident of their ability to hold their own, they also received food, water and moral support from local residents, many of whom joined them. On Sunday, however, a British officer under a flag of truce brought them the notice that Perse had given the

---

[98] The 1798 Rebellion was organized by the United Irishmen, led by several important Protestant nationalists, and a Catholic priest by the name of John Murphy. The aim was to unite Catholics, Anglicans, and Presbyterians to provide a united front to overthrow British rule in Ireland. The uprising was supposed to take place simultaneously across Ireland but due to poor communications, most of the substantial fighting took place in County Wexford, where Father John Murphy had reluctantly taken up arms to help protect his parishioners from the brutality of the British Army. Fighting mostly with pikes and antiquated rifles the rebels were torn about by British artillery. The rebels were all executed. Father Murphy was captured a month or so later. He was stripped, flogged, and hanged. His head was cut off and placed on a spike, and his corpse burnt in a barrel of tar opposite a Catholic church. The British soldiers forced the Catholics in the area to open their windows so they could smell the burning corpse.

order for all rebel troops to surrender. Refusing to believe it, two Volunteers agreed to accompany the British officer to Arbour Hill Prison where Pearse confirmed the surrender order. He suggested that rather than surrender their arms they have the men hide them, saying that they would be needed later.

Fig. 34. Úna Brennan, one of the three women who raised the flag in Enniscorthy, County Wexford, on Easter Monday. Photo taken during a visit to the US in 1945. Photographer unknown.

COUNTY CORK

In County Cork, 1,200 Volunteers commanded by Tomás MacCurtain mustered on Easter Sunday, but they dispersed on Wednesday after receiving contradictory orders by dispatch from the Volunteer leadership in Dublin. At their Sheares Street headquarters, some of the Volunteers engaged in an exchange of rifle fire with British forces. The local clergy met with MacCurtain and convinced him that further resistance would cause civilian deaths. And with misgivings, he finally agreed to surrender his men's arms to the British.[99]

---

[99] Townshend, *op.cit.*, 235.

Meanwhile, the Kent brothers (Thomas, David, Richard and young William) in Fermoy were unconvinced. The four brothers had long been active in the Local Volunteers and were totally committed to the cause, as was their mother, a fierce advocate for Irish independence. They stashed their weapons to wait for another opportunity. The next news that arrived was a rumor that on Saturday, Pearse had surrendered. By May 1, having had no official confirmation, they still believed the Rising was on. When the RIC surrounded their home and demanded their surrender, they replied defiantly, "We are soldiers of the Irish Republic and there is no surrender!"[100] The Kent brothers opened fire with rifles and shotguns. David Kent was shot twice, one in the side and once in the hand losing two fingers. When the head constable demanded their surrender, they opened fire again, killing him and wounding several others. Their bold mother, according to William Kent, "all during the ensuing fight assisted by loading weapons and words of encouragement."[101] When British soldiers arrived to reinforce the RIC, they were resisted as well, and a gun battle continued raging for over three hours until they ran out of ammunition. Richard Kent was shot and killed as he attempted to escape. Thomas and William were captured, and Thomas was sentenced to death and executed by a firing squad from a naval detachment. William was acquitted due to his youth and the intervention of a local priest. It is he who testified before the Bureau of Military History in 1947 about the fate of the last brother, David, who had been wounded and then sentenced to imprisonment.

Arrangements were made for David's trial at Cork Detention Barracks, but an order came from the British Government that the trial be transferred to Richmond Barracks, Dublin. He was tried there on 14th June by a British Military Court-martial, presided over by Lord Chelsemore.

[100] Statement of William Kent, Bureau of Military History (https://www.militaryarchives.ie/collections/online-collections/bureau-of-military-history-1913-1921/reels/bmh/BMH.WS0075.pdf. Accessed Mar. 23, 2021.)
[101] Ibid.

He was ably defended by Mr. Patrick Lynch, K.C. After a prolonged hearing he was found guilty and sentenced to death, the sentence being subsequently commuted to penal servitude for life. He was sent to Dartmoor Prison and later transferred to Pentonville, from which he was released with other I.R.A. prisoners in the general amnesty. While he was in prison his mother died, and on his return home his health was greatly impaired. He was elected T.D. on the Sinn Fein ticket for the East Cork Constituency. He never took his seat in the Dáil as he refused to take the Oath of Allegiance.... He was sent to America on a mission of propaganda on behalf of the I.R.A. He returned home after some months far poorer in health, and, after a life of struggle for the freedom of his country, this brave soldier and patriot died at his home at Bawnard on the 16th November, 1930. His work for the nation he never relinquished until he died, and he died as he had lived, uncompromised and uncompromising, a faithful soldier of the Irish Republic, It was written of the Kent family then, "No threat could bend them, no force could break them/ No wiles could lure them from, the road of right./True men loyal to the cause of Éireann, Soldiers fearless in the fiercest fight;/ From early boyhood through the years of manhood/ On the march to liberty their lives were spent./ God grant to Erin in her day of danger/Guards unwavering as the brothers Kent."[102]

COUNTY KERRY

Tralee Bay in Kerry was chosen as the destination for the landing of the guns and ammunition aboard the *Aud-Norge*, and those weapons were to be distributed across the southwest and west by Kerry Volunteers. The failed attempt to land those arms and the scuttling of the ship was a harsh blow. The problem was compounded by the arrival of Roger Casement at Banna Strand on Good Friday and his subsequent capture, as well as the drowning near Killorglin later that night of three men, Con Keating, Daniel Sheehan and Charles

[102] Ibid.

Monahan, who had attempted to seize radio transmitters from Ca-hersiveen. Nevertheless, there were sufficient Volunteers in the Kerry Brigade to overcome the Constabulary and rescue Casement and his companion, and they were quite willing to do so, but they had been ordered by the Dublin leadership to stand down and do nothing. Not a gun should be fired until the actual Rising lest they tip their hand too early. The following day, when informed of the latest news, Eoin MacNeill called off the Rising planned for Eas-ter Sunday and ordered the Volunteers not to muster. Receiving no countermanding orders, the Volunteers saw no action in Kerry during Easter week. In Dublin, however, there were several Kerry men and women who took part in the Rising as part of the new Army of the Irish Republic.[103]

COUNTIES LAOIS AND LOWTH AND OTHERS

On Easter Sunday in County Laois, Volunteers destroyed a railroad track at Clonadadoran to prevent British troops from reaching Dub-lin from the direction of Wexford. This is believed to be the first action of the Rising, albeit a day ahead of the actual declaration of hostilities. They also destroyed tracks on the Carlow-Kildare line, and one Volunteer carried out a raid on the Wolfhill police barracks.

In County Louth, a small contingent of 28 men had mustered, but then received the countermanding order. Finally, when Peace's dispatch arrived, Commandant Dan Hannigan proclaimed the Irish Republic in the town square and ordered the 12 officers in the RIC barracks to surrender, and they did so without resistance. They also arrested several British officers passing in cars. Some Volunteers then headed to Dublin, among them Sean McEntee who fought at the GPO. Others had arranged to meet up with Thomas Ashe's Fin-

[103] See also, Bridget McAuliffe, Mary McAuliffe, and Owen O'Shea, eds. *Kerry, 1916, Histories and Legacies of the Easter Rising – A Centenary Record* (Tralee: Irish Historical Publications, 2016).

gal Battalion nearby but, by the time they got there, Ashe's forces had surrendered.

There were other small-scale incidents in Tipperary, Belfast, Derry and Tyrone which had no impact. In Counties Limerick and Clare, there were assemblies of Volunteers, but no action was taken when the order from Eoin MacNeill came to stand down.

25

THE DEATH SENTENCES
AND IMPRISONMENTS

There were 3,430 men arrested and 79 women.[104] Of these, 127 were tried and 90 were sentenced to death, including Countess Markiewicz. The executions were extended over a period of ten days (from May 3-12). As the deaths mounted, public opinion, which at first was fixed, began to solidify against the British for prolonged cruelty and retribution upon the Irish populations rather than fair-minded justice. This was further confirmed when it became clear that some who were not active leaders in the Rising or signatories of the proclamation were being marked for death.

MAY 3. Pádraic Perse effectively signed his own death warrant. He was the commander general of the Irish forces, the one who read the Proclamation publicly, but even more significantly, in a letter to his mother, he specifically referred to collaboration with Germany during wartime. In a postscript in a letter to his mother from a prison cell at the Arbour Hill Barracks, he wrote, "P.S. I understand that the German expedition which I was counting on actually set sail but was defeated by the British."[105] The prosecution used this as evidence that would result in a charge of "assisting his Majesty's

---

[104] Some sources say only 77 women were arrested but that is according to the Gifford records. At least two women were arrested and then released as was noted in the case of Elizabeth O'Farrell and Margaret Skinnider. The 77 refers to those actually recoded as being detained in the Richmond Barracks following the Rising. See "A list of women who were detained at Richmond Barracks after the 1916 Rising", *Richmond Barracks* (https://www.richmondbarracks.ie/women-1916/women-detainees-list/, accessed Apr. 2, 2021).

[105] Pádraic Pearse, "Letter to his Mother, May 1, 1916", on Wikisource (https://en.m.wikisource.org/wiki/Patrick_Pearse%E2%80%99_Letter_to_his_Mother,_1_May,_1916, accessed Apr. 2, 2021).

enemies in time of war" which was punishable by death. While this was certainly not the only piece of evidence, it was clearly one which was used to confirm the sentence of death. He was executed on May 3 along with Thomas MacDonagh and Thomas Clarke. Both Clarke and MacDonagh were signatories and held leadership positions.

What is most unusual, though, is that Clarke, like Eamon de Valera, was a US citizen, but only Clarke was put to death.

MAY 4. The following day, Joseph Plunkett, Willie Pearse, Edward Daly and Michael O'Handrahan were put to death. **EDWARD DALY** was a battalion commander and actively engaged in combat at the Four Courts which saw much of the harshest fighting. **MICHAEL O'HANDRAHAN** was second in command under MacDonagh at Jacob's Biscuit Factory. All of those deaths might have been justified by the British.[106]

JOSEPH PLUNKETT, while he had signed the Proclamation and was present at the GPO, had not been active in combat due to very poor health, recovering from neck surgery. His death seemed unnecessary. Seven hours before he was to die, he married his childhood sweetheart Grace Gifford in Kilmainham Gaol. She had earlier converted to Catholicism, and they were to be married on Easter Sunday. The wedding had been postponed by the Rising. Grace never remarried after Joseph's untimely death at age 28.

The execution of **WILLIE PEARSE**, the younger brother of Pádraic, likewise seemed to be motivated by retribution rather than even-handed justice. He was not a commander, nor a signatory to the Proclamation, nor was there any record of him shooting anyone.

MAY 5. JOHN MACBRIDE had fought against the British in the Boer War in South Africa where he had worked as a mine operator, so it

---

[106] That the accused committed an act, to wit, did take part in an armed rebellion and in the waging of war against His Majesty the King, such act being of such a nature as to be calculated to be prejudicial to the Defence to the Realm and being done with the intention and for the purpose of assisting the enemy.

was probably foreordained that he should be hated by the British, especially General John Maxwell who was a commander in that war. That may indeed have been the reason that a day was set aside for his execution. He was also a fervent Irish nationalist and married to the beautiful and brilliant Maud Gonne, the woman beloved by Irish poet William Butler Yeats.

Ironically, his participation in the Rising was a last-minute decision. He was going to meet his brother who was planning to get married and ran into some men who informed him of the activities on Easter Monday. Knowing that it was ill-planned and doubtful of success, he was nevertheless determined to accompany his comrades and joined the battalion at Jacob's Biscuit Factory. When they were called upon to surrender at the end of the week, he and several others were given an opportunity by Commander MacDonagh to escape with their arms to fight another day. However, although several took advantage of the opportunity, MacBride felt it was dishonorable to do so.

At 3.40am on May 5, when they came to take him away, he requested that he not be blindfolded or handcuffed, but the British refused to give him that bit of respect. As he stood before the firing squad he said: "Then, fire away. I have been looking down the barrels of rifles all my life."[107]

8 MAY. ÉAMONN CEANNT was part of the IRB Military Council which planned the Rising, a signer of the Proclamation, and Commander of the 4th Battalion. He had commanded units at the South Dublin Union and the Marrowbone Lane Distillery. He was unquestionably one of the major leaders of the Rising. When the surrender order came from Pearse he was very reluctant to have his soldiers lay down their arms. His units had been quite successful in very intense battles against the British and were not defeated. He felt that the order was premature. Ultimately, he agreed, both because

---

[107] Dermot McEvoy, "On This Day: Easter Rising leader John MacBride executed in 1916", May 5, 2021 on Irish Central (https://www.irishcentral.com/roots/history/john-macbride-easter-rising, accessed Apr. 3, 2021).

he felt obliged to obey an order from a superior and because he assumed it was a negotiated surrender to save civilian lives. Too late he discovered that Pearse had surrendered all of the rebel forces unconditionally. Before his death Ceannt wrote, "I leave for the guidance of other Irish Revolutionaries who may tread the path which I have trod, this advice: never to treat with the enemy, never to surrender at his mercy..."[108]

SÉAN HEUSTON was a member of the Fianna Éireann, one of the capable young men who worked alongside Countess Markiewicz drilling and training teenage recruits. He also taught them Irish language and history. In 1916 he was a vice-commandant of the Dublin Battalion under James Connolly. He was assigned to hold the Mendicity Institute for three to four hours to give Pearse, Connolly and others time to set up headquarters in the GPO and prepare the defenses. Heuston and his men managed to hold out for two days despite fearsome attacks from 300 British troops heavily armed not only with superior Enfield rifles but Maxim machine guns. Finally with the British closing in and tossing grenades into the building, trapped with several men badly wounded, Heuston surrendered his hopelessly outnumbered force.

According to Seamus Brennan, a Volunteer captured that day, the British "were infuriated when they saw the pygmy forces that had given them such a stuff battle and caused them so many casualties... In the (Royal) Barracks we were lined up on the parade ground. Here we were attacked by British soldiers, kicked, beaten, spat upon."[109] Heuston was transferred to the Richmond Barracks for court martial on May 4 and executed on May 8 at dawn. He was 25 years old.

MICHAEL MALLIN, the commandant of the Irish Citizen Army fighting at St. Stephen's Green and later at the College of Surgeons, was an active combatant and an effective strategist. However, by Thursday his garrison at the College was cut off from the rebel

---

[108] "Eamonn Ceannt's Last Message", *Irish Independent*, Jul. 9, 1926.
[109] Piaras MacLochlainn, *Last Words, Letters And Statements Of The Leaders Executed After The Rising of Easter 1916* (Dublin: Kilmainham Jail Restoration Society, 1971).

headquarters and had begun to run out of ammunition and food. On Sunday, April 30, he received the surrender order from Pearse, co-signed by Connolly. The note was delivered to Countess Markiewicz because Mallin was in another part of the building. She passed it on to Mallin. With his troops exhausted, hungry and out of ammunition, he saw no other option. He surrendered to Captain Courcy-Wheeler, General Lowe's adjutant.

As a former British officer, it was clear that the president of the court martial and his staff were out to humiliate Mallin. They not only refused to include statements made by him but provided written notations in the record implying things he did not say. This was later confirmed by Captain Courcy-Wheeler when he read the transcript. One of the most distressing was the suggestion that Mallin implicated Countess Markiewicz as the major strategist and co-commander of his unit in an effort to avoid the death penalty. This is patently absurd. Mallin had accepted his certain death and knew that he would receive no mercy from his former fellow officers. The notations in the record were made by the president of the court martial, likely at the instruction of General Maxwell who had contempt both for Mallin joining the Irish cause, and for Markiewicz's participation as an active combatant. The former had left the British Army and the latter had left the ranks of the Anglo-Irish Ascendancy. Both actions enraged General Maxwell's sense of propriety. He had earlier said, "that woman is bloody guilty and dangerous. She is a woman who has forfeited the privileges of her sex." [110]He urged most strongly that she be put to death.

CORNELIUS (CON) COLBERT was a former Fianna scout who served under Captain Seamus Murphy at the Marrowbone Lane Distillery. Murphy's Volunteers acquitted themselves well in this position and, when the British withdrew on Saturday morning, felt that they had scored a significant victory. They were dismayed to learn from Thomas MacDonagh on Sunday that Pearse had ordered all rebel troops to surrender. Murphy and his men stacked their

---

[110] Quoted in *Townshend, Easter, 1916*, 286.

arms in St. Patrick's Park and then were marched under escort to Richmond Barracks. Although Murphy was the commandant of the group, he was unknown to the British, and was passed over and ultimately deported. Colbert, however, was singled out because of his public drilling of the Fianna boys and his tearing down of the Union Jack during anti-conscription protests. He was sentenced to death at his court martial. Although he was unfairly singled out, he had no bitterness. On the eve of his execution, he was visited by Captain Murphy's wife. He said to her: "I am one of the lucky ones. I am proud to die for such a cause." He then cut the brass button from his tunic and gave them to her as mementos, saying, "I will be passing away at the dawning of the day."[111]

9 MAY. THOMAS KENT was arrested in Cork following a raid by the Royal Irish Constabulary, after a misguided effort to confiscate weapons during which his brother was fatally wounded. He was executed at dawn on May 9, 1916 in Fermoy, County Cork. His death caused a bit of an uproar since he was not part of the Dublin forces, and not really a part of the Rising since he and his Volunteers received news to stand down earlier in the week.

When news of the execution reached John Dillon of the Irish Parliamentary Party on May 11 he got up in the House of Commons and let loose: "I have received word that a man named Kent has been executed in Fermoy, which is the first execution that has taken place outside Dublin. The fact is one that will create a very grave shock in Ireland. Because it looks like a roving commission to carry these horrible executions all over the country. This, I say, was the first execution outside the city of Dublin. In a district where there have been no serious disturbances."

Dillon then turned his wrath on General Maxwell: "Would not any sensible statesman think he had enough to do in Dublin and the other centers where disturbance broke out without doing ev-

---

[111] Dermot McEvoy, "On This Day: Easter Rising leader Con Colbert was executed", *Irish Central,* May 8, 2021 (https://www.irishcentral.com/roots/history/con-colbert-1916-easter-rising, accessed Apr. 14, 2021).

erything possible to raise disturbance and spread disaffection over the whole country?"

Dillon then dug into the Prime Minister, Asquith: "You are letting loose a river of blood and make no mistake about it, between two races who, after three hundred years of hatred and of strife, we have nearly succeeded in bringing together."[112]

12 MAY. SÉAN MACDERMOTT (Sean MacDiarmada) was one of the main organizers of the Rising and had signed the Proclamation. As a member of the Military Council of the Irish Republican Brotherhood, he was instrumental, along with Thomas Clarke, in the planning and in the decision to go ahead in spite of the countermanding order to stand down on Easter Sunday. MacDermott believed that a "blood sacrifice"[113] was necessary to preserve the Irish identity which was slowly being eroded by submission to Britain. He was active in several organizations dedicated to Irish culture, Irish language, and Irish independence including the Gaelic League, Sinn Fein, and the Ancient Order of Hibernians. MacDermott had been stricken with polio at the age of 27 and walked with a cane. Due to his disability, he did not actively engage in combat during the Rising but was present in the GPO along with Clarke, Connolly and Pearse, and contributed to the strategy. After the surrender he sent letters to Nell Ryan, a leader of the Wexford branch of the Cumann na mBan, whose sisters Phyllis and Josephine had served as couriers in the GPO. He and Josephine, known as Min, were engaged to be married. She was the last person to visit him before his execution in the early morning hours of May 12. His last words were, "I die that the Irish nation might live." In his hometown today, a statue engraved with those words honors his memory.

[112] Dermot McEvoy, "On This Day: 1916 Easter Rising leader Thomas Kent executed", *Irish Central*, May 9, 2021 (https://www.irishcentral.com/roots/history/1916-easter-rising-thomas-kent-executed, accessed April 14, 2021).

[113] Donal Fallon, "Putting the language of Pearse in context: Blood Sacrifice and 1916", *Independent.ie*, Apr. 10, 2016 (https://www.independent.ie/irish-news/1916/rising-perspectives/putting-the-language-of-pearse-in-context-blood-sacrifice-and-1916-34611012.html, accessed May 1, 2021).

JAMES CONNOLLY was still suffering from his wounds after the surrender. The doctors predicted he would likely die from his wounds, one of which had become gangrenous. He was clearly suffering alone in the makeshift hospital room at Dublin Castle where he was being held prisoner. As Nora Connolly recalls

> The next 12 days or so were the days of anguish and heartbreak, waiting and hoping. Day, after day, came news of the executions, and we wondered when they would stop; would Daddy be executed in his wounded condition? When we did get in to see him, Daddy had not much hope.

When she and her sister at last got to see him, their meeting was poignant. Despite his injuries and imminent death, he was still concerned with the outcome of the Rising and the fate of the men.

One of the first questions Daddy asked me, was, "What happened in the North?" "It was no use, Daddy, the men were all dispersed and couldn't be brought together again. I did my best, I waited and waited. When I saw there would be no fighting there, I made my way back to Dublin, but the fighting was over when I arrived here. I had no chance, Daddy, I did nothing."

"I think my little woman did as much as anyone," he said, as he drew my head down to his breast. At 12 o'clock on Thursday night, 11th May 1916, we saw him for the last time and as I kissed Daddy, he held me close to him and said, "I'm proud of you Nora girl."[114]

> On the morning of May 12, he was carried by stretcher to Kilmainham Gaol. There he was propped up in a chair against a wall, then strapped in to stay upright so that he could be easily shot by the firing squad. Previously agnostic for many years, at this time he affirmed his Catholic faith, received the last rites of the Church and absolution, and said a prayer for those about to shoot him. The bullets tore into his breast and neck, and he slumped forward. The doctor in attendance pronounced

[114] Statement by Mrs. Nora Connolly O'Brien, Bureau of Military History. (https://www.militaryarchives.ie/collections/online-collections/bureau-of-military-history-1913-1921/reels/bmh/BMH.WS0286.pdf, accessed May 1, 2021).

him dead and his body was dumped into a mass grave with no coffin. Quicklime was shoveled over it.

The manner of his execution was widely reported even by neutral witnesses as being particularly cruel and heartless. It was the cause of much anger in Ireland even among people who had not supported the Rising. It also drew a great deal of attention in the US where the press (usually sympathetic to Britain) were appalled at the continued executions and reflected the views of many Irish Americans especially in cities like Boston, Philadelphia, Chicago, and New York.

LEADERS WHO MANAGED TO EVADE DEATH

MICHAEL COLLINS AND EAMON DE VALERA both lived to make a major impact on later Irish history, and *Constance Markiewicz* became a forceful legislator in the Irish government. Their escapes from death were fortuitous.

MICHAEL COLLINS was a minor figure in the Rising, but his fame became worldwide after the 1993 eponymous film starring Liam Neeson. The movie featured Collins' later exploits after he fortuitously escaped execution after the Rising. During the 1916 Rising he had served as an aide-de-camp to Joseph Plunkett and was instrumental in leading the evacuation from the GPO. After the surrender he was taken to Dublin's Richmond Barracks and during the screening was identified as someone who should be selected for further interrogation. However, when he heard his name being called out, he moved to the other side of the building where a group of prisoners were being transferred to another prison. He went with that group and was shipped to the Frongoch internment camp in Wales. There, he emerged as the organizer of planned protests and non-cooperation with authorities. His activities in the camp provided him with connections to republicans from all over Ireland

and honed his leadership skills. Upon his release, he would become a thorn in the side of the British Army.[115]

EAMON DE VALERA was one of the last to be considered for execution. There were several reasons. First, his group was the last to be taken into custody. They did not receive the surrender order until 24 hours after the main group of rebels had surrendered. Then he and his men were held at Bullsbridge for two days until they were marched to Richmond Barracks on May 3. The screening of leaders for the courts martial had already occurred and the first group of executions had already taken place. De Valera was not one of the signers of the Proclamation, nor one of the IRB planners, so his name did not come up.

Second, his wife Sinead had contacted the US consul in Dublin and brought to his attention that fact that de Valera was a US citizen. In addition, his half-brother in New York had contacted a senior official in Dublin Castle and made a similar representation. Meanwhile public reaction to the executions had already begun and in the US the death of Thomas Clarke, an American citizen, had caused outrage among many readers, especially Irish Americans.

Third, after the execution of James Connolly on May 12, General Maxwell asked William Wiley, the prosecuting officer, who was next. When Wiley told him it was de Valera, Maxwell asked if he was someone important. Wiley replied, "No. He is a school master who was taken at Boland's Mill."[116] These factors combined led to his life being spared, another future leader of the Republic who would return to plague the British after a brief term in prison.

CONSTANCE MARKIEWICZ. Although she was convicted of leading an insurrection and sentenced to death, her sister Eva Gore-Booth led an intense campaign to have her death sentence vacated. A well-known London intellectual and magazine editor,

---

[115] Tim Pat Coogan, *Michael Collins, A Biography* (London: Arrow Books, Ltd., 1991), 50.
[116] Ronan Fanning, *Eamon de Valera: A Will to Power* (London: Faber & Faber, 2015), extracted at Independent.ie, Mar. 3, 2016 (https://www.independent.ie/irish-news/1916/the-rising-explained/how-dev-escaped-execution-in-1916-34495475.html, accessed May 12, 2021).

Gore-Booth had considerable influence both in England and abroad. She traveled to Dublin and met with the authorities there as well. Eventually the sentence was commuted to penal servitude for life at Aylesbury Prison. When informed of the decision of the courts martial, Markiewicz reputedly said to the British officer who brought the news, "I wish your lot had the decency to shoot me."[117]

Indeed, the British may have subsequently wished they had. She was released in the general amnesty of 1917, and subsequently appointed to the executive committee of Sinn Fein. Almost immediately, she was arrested again for campaigning against the conscription of Irish boys into the English Army.

While in prison she ran as a Parliamentary candidate from the St. Patrick's Division of Dublin in the 1918 general election. However, although elected, she did not take her seat. Released from prison again in 1919, she was arrested once again for giving a seditious speech. Four months later this was followed by another arrest and two-year sentence to hard labor. She was finally released again by the general amnesty which followed the signing of the Irish Peace Treaty and elected to the Irish Free State Parliament in 1923.

AUGUST 3. THE LAST TO DIE

The first supporter of Irish nationalism captured by the British for his activities, and the last to die, was **SIR ROGER CASEMENT**, a champion of human rights in South America and Africa who was knighted by the King for his services in the Congo. Casement was arrested on Banna Strand, Tralee Bay, County Kerry for his part in arranging the purchase of German guns and ammunition for the rebels. Although the weapons never reached the rebels and the ship was scuttled when intercepted by a British patrol, he was nonetheless charged with treason. He was the last of the heroes of the Rising to give his life to the cause.

---

[117] Colin Flint (ed.), *The Geography of War and Peace: From Death Camps to Diplomacy* (New York: Oxford University Press, 2005), 144.

Fig. 35. "Commutation of Death Sentence on Rebel Countess." *Daily Mirror* (London), May 8, 1916.

Given his outstanding service to the British Empire and his international reputation for integrity, courage and the pursuit of social justice, not even the prosecution wished to see him hanged. But that was the prescribed penalty for an English citizen convicted of treason. The prosecutor suggested to Casement's barrister that he plead "guilty but insane" and thus avoid the noose. When presented with this option, Casement proudly refused. After a trial held from June 26-29, he was found guilty of treason, stripped of his knighthood, and was sentenced to death.

Many dignitaries around the world appealed for clemency, including Arthur Conan Doyle, William Butler Yeats, and George Bernard Shaw. The United States Senate formally joined as an *amicus curiae* in the appeal of his death sentence. All to no avail. He was hanged at Pentonville Prison on August 3, 1916.

Casement's body was buried in the prison graveyard and covered with quicklime. After the establishment of the Irish Republic, Eamon de Valera visited Winston Churchill, the Prime Minister, and formally requested that Casement's remains be returned to Ireland. The request was denied. Finally, during the administration of Harold Wilson in 1965 the request was granted, and the body of Sir Roger Casement was returned to Ireland and buried with full military honors in Glasnevin Cemetery in Dublin.[118]

IMPRISONMENTS

In the immediate aftermath of the Rising the authorities arrested 3,430 men and 79 women thought to be "Sinn Feiners". The accuracy of the intelligence on which the arrests were based can be judged from the facts that 1,424 were released within a fortnight and that all but 579 were subsequently released as posing no danger to the state.

Even some of those who were deported, along with the veterans of the Rising, to English prisons and the Frongoch internment camp in Wales had no previous involvement in violent nationalism. In addition, after the initial confinement of 77 women in Kilmainham Gaol, 12 of these were sent for longer terms to Mountjoy Prison,

[118] Scott Wilson, *Resting Places: The Burial Sites of More Than 14,000 Famous Persons* (New York: McFarland & Company, 2016), Kindle Edition, loc 7669.

and six of them ultimately deported to England[119] to British maximum-security facilities which further incensed public opinion both in Ireland and abroad. To make sure that the fate of these prisoners, as well as the brutal deaths of Francis Sheehy-Skeffington and James Connolly were made public several veterans of the Rising including Nora Connolly, Hanna Sheehy-Skeffington, Nellie Gifford and others went to the US, described the British atrocities to packed crowds of Irish Americans, and raised funds for the republican cause and the continuing struggle for independence.

Fig. 36. Kilmainham Gaol where many
of the Irish revolutionaries were imprisoned.

[119] Winnifred Carney, Bridget Foley, Helena Molony and Constance Markiewicz to Aylesbury Prison; Elizabeth Lynn to Bath Prison; Nell Ryan and Marie Perolz to Lewes Prison. Bureau of Military History. Deportations. BMH.WS1698 PART 2.pdf, on page 176.

26
AFTERMATH: TWO MORE WARS

Public opinion in Ireland had been mixed during the actual Rising. Some believed that the revolt was ill-conceived; others felt they should support the British Army in the war against Germany (for which some were receiving support payments from Irish volunteers serving abroad). Many in the north were opposed to an independent Republic, preferring the economic benefits as well as the Protestantism of Ulster; others saw an opportunity to enrich themselves through looting during the chaos. Those fully committed to the Nationalist cause were probably not as prevalent as those who were undecided and wavering. But the civilian deaths caused by British recklessness and indifference, the drawn-out executions of the Rising leaders, the murder of innocents on North King Street and of Sheehy-Skeffington, galvanized support for independence. The solidarity of more than nine million people Irish-born or of Irish descent living abroad, especially in the US, would provide both moral and financial support.

A darkness of cruelty, destruction and death, unimagined by either side of the Irish question was about to descend on the country like the blackness of an India inkwell. A downward spiral was beginning, to the seventh circle of Dante's hell where indiscriminate violence would be the order of the day in the War of Independence, before treachery would rear its ugly head in a fraternal "civil" war. Few saw the violence coming and it began on what seemed to the English to be a positive note.

The British Parliament could not ignore the movement for Irish self-government and in 1918 decided to finally implement Home Rule. They made the unfortunate mistake, however, of coupling that decision with a new conscription policy. Not only had the war in Europe become unpopular with the families of the thousands of young Irish boys killed, but it was an insult to those whose sons had volunteered to fight to now make service mandatory especially for a people who had been oppressed and whose leaders had been put to death. Massive protests against conscription took place.

When elections were held for Parliament in 1918, 73 out of 105 Irish representatives belonged to Sinn Fein, the nationalist party. Many of the newly-elected members, including Countess Markiewicz, the first woman to be elected, refused to take their seats. Instead, they set up an Irish Parliament known as the First Dáil,[120] consisting exclusively of Sinn Fein members. They also issued a "Declaration of Independence to All the Nations of the World" reaffirming the Proclamation of 1916 establishing an Irish Republic. The Irish Volunteers and the ICA had merged into the Army of the Republic in 1916 and was now more commonly known as the Irish Republican Army (IRA). By January 1919, many of their members were involved in an undeclared guerrilla war against the British-controlled Royal Irish Constabulary, the Dublin Metropolitan Police, and troops that supported them. As the undeclared war progressed, especially in the countryside, two British paramilitary forces emerged. One was a group of World War I veterans called the Black and Tans. The other was called the Auxiliary Division and was composed chiefly of former officers of the British Army known as the "Auxies." The two groups worked in concert and were notorious for their cruelty, their destruction of private property, burning of houses, and rapaciousness. Their reputation for brutality and reprisal against Irish citizens has been well-documented and served to harden Irish resistance.

Meanwhile in Dublin, leaders went ahead and organized the new Irish government. In 1920 the British government introduced another bill to create two devolved governments: one for the six northern counties (Northern Ireland) and one for the rest of the island (Southern Ireland). While the leaders of Ulster immediately

[120] "Wars and Conflicts: 1916 Easter Rising – Aftermath", *BBC History* (http://www.bbc.co.uk/history/british/easterrising/aftermath/af01.shtml, accessed May 15, 2021).

proceeded to join the new British-conceived dominion, the leaders of the Irish Republic refused, and proceeded with their own independent government. In July of 1920 both sides declared a ceasefire, but sporadic fighting continued well into 1921.

Known as the War of Independence (1919-21) this conflict ostensibly ended when the Anglo-Irish Treaty, signed by Michael Collins, was confirmed by the Dáil Érieann by a vote of 64-57. However, there were major problems with the Treaty and the acts which followed. First, de Valera resigned as President of the Republic, arguing that the Dáil did not have the authority to approve the treaty and that its members were breaking their oath to the Irish Republic. Second, the Treaty required an oath of allegiance to the crown. Third, there would be essentially two protectorates, one in the north and one in the south, each under the British Crown like Australia and Canada. While the descendants of English colonists in the north, mostly Protestant, were amenable, Eamon de Valera and the many Catholic members of the new Irish Republic had no intention of submitting. Others in the south, including Collins who had hoped to end the conflict by a compromise, felt betrayed by this decision to withdraw, since it was de Valera himself who sent Collins to London to negotiate. This conflict between friends and fellow officers of the earlier Rising and the War of Independence led to fighting between anti-Treaty forces and the newly elected Irish government, called the Irish Free State, a self-governing member of the British Commonwealth. It was known as the Irish Civil War (1921-1923) which ended in victory for the newly named National Army over the anti-Treaty IRA forces.[121] Both, ironically, were composed of former members of the IRA.

Finally, in 1949, a coalition government containing elements of both sides in the Civil War (pro-Treaty and anti-Treaty) left the British Commonwealth and declared the Republic of Ireland. The fly in the ointment, however, was the partition which still left Northern Ireland separated from the Republic. Northern Ireland was largely

---

[121] While both armies were composed of former IRA soldiers, only the anti-Treaty forces retained the name.

loyalist and Protestant but contained a Catholic minority in Derry which were deprived of civil rights. Unwilling to take an oath of allegiance, they were not allowed to work in sought-after positions such as those in the shipyards in Belfast. In addition, they were subjected to invasive commemorations on King Billy Day[122] when Protestant Orangeman marched with deafening Lambeg drums in celebration of King William's seventeenth-century conquest of the region purposely provoking the Catholic residents. Derry was a time bomb which would erupt in violence and another Bloody Sunday 20 years later.

Fig. 37. King Billy Day in Derry with enormous drums beating like thunder in the narrow streets, and a banner (partially visible) depicting King William on a white stallion and the words "In glorious memory."

[122] The Orange Order, a fraternal Protestant group which includes many of the Northern Ireland leadership celebrate the Battle of the Boyne (July 11, 1690) when the Catholic English King James II was defeated by William of Orange, a Dutch prince. He was married to Mary, a potential heiress to the British throne, hence, William and Mary. They were both Protestants and promised to restore the rights and privileges of their co-religionists as well as provide settlements and land grants to their supporters. Also, while the battle was on July 11, the event is celebrated on July 12.

27
WOMEN LEADERS AFTER THE RISING

MARY SPRING RICE

After her hazardous 23-day voyage with Molly Childers in the *Asgard* bringing rifles and ammunition to the Irish Volunteers at Howth, Mary Spring Rice continued to support the rebel cause but with a low profile. In fact, shortly after the Howth landing, she was seen at the upscale Dublin Club having tea. As a member of the Anglo-Irish aristocracy, she was never bothered by the authorities, although it is likely she was suspected to be a sympathizer, as the report of her at the club indicates. Her cousin, Sir Arthur Cecil Spring Rice, was Britain's ambassador to the US during World War I and a close friend of Teddy Roosevelt.[123] That connection likely proved a valuable protection.

During the War of Independence (1919-21) she supported the nationalist cause, trained first aid workers, nursed wounded volunteers, and lent her boat, the *Santa Cruz*, to Republicans to carry messages, weapons, and supplies. She died of tuberculosis at a sanitarium in Wales in 1929. At her funeral, her coffin was draped in the Irish flag, and she had an honor guard consisting of members of the Irish Republican Army and the Gaelic League.[124]

---

[123] Grant Carlson, "Roosevelt's Contemporaries: Cecil Spring Rice" on the website of the Theodore Roosevelt Center at Dickinson State University, Apr. 7 2014 (https://www.theodorerooseveltcenter.org/Blog/Item/Cecil%20Spring%20Rice, accessed May 8, 2021).
See also David Henry Burton. *Cecil Spring Rice: A Diplomat's Life* (Vancouver: Fairleigh University Press, 1990).
[124] *Limerick Leader,* December 13, 1924.

MOLLY CHILDERS. Molly Childers, the intrepid wife of author Erskine Childers, who helped pilot the *Asgard* loaded with rifles to Howth Harbor along with Mary Spring Rice, applied herself to war relief after the Rising. She was particularly involved with the Belgium refugees who were left homeless and in terrible camps, often without sufficient food, shelter, or medicine. She and her sister raised funds for them and made sure that the money was properly applied to basic needs. King George V conferred on her the prestigious MBE (Member of the British Empire) for this work.[125] She also received the national medal of Belgium from Queen Elizabeth of that country. She and her husband, along with Maud Gonne, were active in the Irish White Cross, which later became part of the International Red Cross. She was also a member of the Women's International League for Peace and Freedom which was a forerunner of UNESCO. Much of her time was also devoted to her son's education.

While her husband grew more active in Irish politics after the Rising, Molly worked as a writer and fill-in publisher of the *Irish Bulletin*, the official gazette of the government of the Irish Republic. She also catered to foreign journalists and worked closely with Minister for Finance Michael Collins, managing and distributing monies raised by the Dáil Éireann Loan that amounted to approximately £350,000. Erskine became a Sinn Fein candidate for office but did not take a seat since he was against the treaty signed by Michael Collins which required Irish leaders to take an oath of allegiance to the British Crown. When the Civil War broke out in 1922 with the Free State (pro-Treaty) and the Sinn Fein (anti-Treaty) forces opposed, Childers and Collins found themselves on opposite sides.

On his way to visit with de Valera, Childers was captured by Free State soldiers. He was charged with possession of an illegal weapon and engaging in anti-government action. Ironically, the pistol he was carrying was a gift from his friend and former comrade, Mi-

---

[125] *The London Gazette*, No. 30460, (3rd Supplement), January 4, 1918, 392.

chael Collins. Childers was sentenced to death. He appealed but the appeal was rejected whereupon Childers made his son promise that he would shake hands and make peace with those who signed his execution orders so that enmity between Irishmen would end in his lifetime. At his death, Eamon de Valera wrote, "He died the Prince he was. Of all the men I ever met, I would say he was the noblest."[126]

Molly was treated quite shabbily after his death. She was unable to access funds from their bank account because the new government did not provide an official death certificate. His effects which included items of "sentimental value including a gold half-hunter watch, a silver cigarette case, and gold cufflinks"[127] were never returned. Nevertheless, Molly remained committed to the Republican cause. In 1926 she was honorary treasurer of the Republican Daily Press Fund established in 1924 to raise funds for a republican newspaper. The resultant Irish Press was published in 1931. She returned to the US briefly for medical treatment in 1947, then returned to Glendalough House in Annamoe, County Wicklow until her death in 1964.[128] She was very proud of her son, who would become in June 1973 the 4th President of the Irish Republic to which she and her husband had dedicated their lives.

ALICE STOPFORD GREEN. The well-known historian, who helped fund the Howth gun purchases, was a close friend of Sir Roger Casement whom she had gotten to know through her work with the Congo Reform Movement. She was one of many influential people who tried to influence the British appeals court in the commutation petition. She was devastated by the court's refusal to commute the death sentence and left London soon after his execution, never to return.

---

[126] Joe Mellor, "The Riddle of Erskine Childers", *The London Economic*, June. 23 2014 (https://www.thelondoneconomic.com/politics/the-riddle-of-erskine-childers-3397/, accessed May 10, 2021).

[127] Ibid.

[128] Tomás Ó Coisdealbha, "Mary (Molly) Alden Osgood Childers (1875-1964)", *Fenian Graves*, Jun. 3, 2014 (https://feniangraves.net/Childers,%20Molly/Molly%20Childers%20bio.htm, accessed May 11, 2021).

Back in Ireland she became active in the movement to promote the Canadian-type dominion status favored by moderates both in the north and south of Ireland. Unlike many others, she decided to support the pro-Treaty side in the Civil War and had Michael Collins as a frequent guest in her home. She believed that, although the Irish Free State was a compromise, it was the best chance of ending the violence. She was the first person to be elected (or appointed) to the Irish Senate (Seanad Éireann) and one of only four women. She served in that post until her death in 1929.[129]

She was the author of eight books. Her last, written in 1925, was *History of the Irish State*. Stepford Rice was a popular intellectual hostess throughout the Roaring Twenties and a respected figure both in Dublin and in the north where she continued to visit with family and friends. She died at the age of 82.

HANNA SHEEHY-SKEFFINGTON. Had always been a leader in promoting women's rights. Early on she saw the connection between national freedom and gender equality even though her father, an ardent nationalist and a politician, had voted against women's suffrage.

Her husband Francis, whom she met in college, was quite different from her father. He was an active feminist and joined her in the founding of the Irish Women's Franchise League in 1908. She herself was one of the founding members of the Irish Women's Workers' Union and was in the forefront of union activities. She was a popular and prolific writer, authoring numerous articles for the *Irish Citizen*, a newspaper she and her husband founded. Ironically both she and Francis were pacifists and, on the day he was captured by the British, he was handing out pamphlets and trying to prevent looting that was occurring in the wake of the Rising. His murder at the hands of a vengeful English officer was not only unjustified but repugnant to all who heard of it.

After the Rising she initiated an inquiry into her husband's death, but the London authorities refused to assign blame or make repara-

---

[129] Roy Johnson, "Century of Endeavor" (1999) on *Internet Archive* (http://www.iol.ie/~rjtechne/century130703/1900s/asgmcd.htm, accessed May 12, 2021).

tions. Infuriated by their callousness, she obtained a false passport and went to America where for 18 months she went on a whirlwind tour, speaking to large crowds in a dozen different cities and venues, including Carnegie Hall in New York, on the evils of British militarism and colonialism, the barbarous treatment of native people in their Empire, and the importance of Irish independence. She created much goodwill toward Ireland from citizens in the US and raised over $40,000 dollars for Michael Collins and the upcoming War of Independence.[130] She even met with President Woodrow Wilson.[131]

After her return to Ireland, she was arrested and transported to London and imprisoned with Countess Markiewicz and others in Holloway Jail. After surviving a dangerous hunger strike, she and the other women with her were released. In May of 1919 she was appointed Organizing Secretary of Sinn Fein, responsible for the organization's propaganda campaign. However, her anti-British speeches during the War of Independence caused her to go on the run to avoid arrest and internment. As Margaret Ward points out in her fine biography, after the Anglo-Irish Treaty was signed in 1921, Hanna along with most of the women of Cumann na mBan rejected the partition of Ireland and refused to accept the oath of allegiance to the British Crown.

When the Civil War broke out, she and several others tried to reconcile the differences between the two factions and stop the fighting but were unsuccessful. She sided with the anti-Treaty group and at de Valera's request visited the US again. This time she and her two companions raised $123,000.[132] In 1926, although initially a part of the executive of the new Fianna Fail party, she saw the writing on the wall and realized that de Valera would begin to compro-

---

[130] $40,000 in 1917 is equivalent in purchasing power to about $827,740.63 today, an increase of $787,740.63 over 104 years.
[131] Margaret Ward, *Fearless Woman: Hanna Sheehy Skeffington, Feminism and the Irish Revolution* (Dublin: Dufour Editions, 2020). Most of the biographical facts are gleaned from this insightful and carefully researched text,
[132] Jim Shaughnessy, "This month in history: Suffragette Hanna Sheehy-Skeffington born in Co Cork", *Irish Central*, Nov. 4, 2019 (https://www.irishcentral.com/roots/history/hanna-sheehy-skeffington, accessed May 14, 2021).

mise to stay in power rather than stand by the principles enunciated in the Proclamation of 1916. She decided to return to the Sinn Fein and the republican cause. She felt that the new government was theocratic and provincial and relegated the role of women to that of domestics. Although she died in 1955, her memory is enshrined in statues, plaques, and even a women's study hall named after her at a Dublin university. Her writings live on as well, not only through citations by scholars or collections by archivists, but also through excerpts in popular works such as Margaret Ward's books on feminism, and biographies of women who contributed to Irish history.

Fig. 38. Cover of Margaret Ward's annotated collection of Hanna Sheehy Skeffington's writings.

MOLLY O'REILLY was the young girl who hoisted the old green and gold flag of ancient Ireland[133] over Liberty Hall on Palm Sunday, a week before the Rising at the request of James Connolly. At age 11 she had first seen Connolly when she was practicing with a group of dancers at Liberty Hall. Later she listened to several of his talks and was inspired to work for social justice. She joined the Irish girl scouts and was drawn to service especially with the needy in the inner city. She was a volunteer during the Dublin lockout and helped organize a food kitchen for the striking workers and their families. In July of 1914 she joined the Irish Citizen Army and was involved in concealing weapons from the Howth landing until they could be funneled to troops in the field.

On Easter Monday she began working as a courier to carry dispatches from the GPO to Liberty Hall and elsewhere, often under heavy fire from rifles and machine guns. She managed to do this for almost the entire week and avoided capture by the enemy. After the Rising she went to Yorkshire where she studied nursing, returning to Ireland in 1919. Once home again, she joined the Cumann na mBan and organized safe houses for the IRA men fighting the Black and Tans. She also worked undercover as a waitress at the British officer's club in St. Stephen's Green to provide Michael Collin (in the IRA Intelligence Office) with details of troop movements and planned Black and Tan raids.

She broke with Collins after his signing of the Treaty of 1921 which she opposed and joined the Republican forces during the Civil War. She was arrested in 1923 and, after nine months in prison, helped organize a hunger strike. After more than two weeks of starvation she and 50 other women and several emaciated and weakened men were released from custody. Like many women involved in the Rising she was less than enthusiastic about the lim-

---

[133] Some sources suggest that it was the flag of the Irish Citizen Army. However, remnants received of the flag after the Rising (and preserved for posterity in the Irish National Museum) indicate that it was the ancient flag (green with the gold harp), not the twentieth-century flag of the ICA designed by James Connolly. For a fuller discussion of Irish flags see Appendix B.

itations of the 1937 Irish Constitution and the compromises of de Valera with the Church which resulted in stifling women's rights. Nonetheless she remained a staunch supporter of the Republic until her death in 1950.

ELIZABETH O'FARRELL courageously walked though enemy fire to deliver Pearse's surrender to the British command and later the subsequent orders to the outlying posts, despite her personal belief that the surrender was premature. She put up with the insults of British soldiers, the disbelief on the part of some post commanders, the insolence of British officers, and the broken word of General Lowe. By sheer persistence, she secured her release and went back to what she knew well, caring for Irish women at their most vulnerable time in life. She also helped as a nurse for the wounded during the Irish War of Independence. After the Treaty of 1921, which she did not support, she absented herself from Irish politics. She worked as a midwife and nurse at the National Maternity Hospital in Dublin for the remainder of her life.

If she had been outraged by the British authorities and their contempt for Irish women, she was also sorely disappointed by the subsequent Irish governments which, as Connolly warned, appeared to have merely substituted one flag for another. She had hoped that the new Irish government would respect women's rights, grant suffrage and equal opportunity, and establish social justice for working men and women. She was sorely disappointed. When approached by the Bureau of Military History which was collecting oral histories of the survivors of the Rising, she said, "All governments since 1921 have betrayed the Republic."[134]

She died unrepentant on June 25, 1957, and is buried next to her lifelong companion, Julia Grenan, in Glasnevin Cemetery.

---

[134] Donal Fallon, "Deported at 92: The inimitable Joe Clarke", *Come Here to Me!*, Dec. 8, 2016 (https://comeheretome.com/2016/12/08/deported-at92-the-inimitable-joe-clarke/, accessed May 13, 2021).

JULIA GRENAN, the intrepid nurse who together with Winnifred Carney and Elizabeth O'Farrell, refused to be evacuated from the GPO when the roof was collapsing and the fires had broken out from artillery and incendiary bombs, was a heroine. When the survivors finally tunneled through to Moore Street, the three women continued to care for the wounded including James Connolly until the final surrender was decided. When O'Farrell delivered the surrender to the British position, ignoring the heavy gun fire around her, protected only by a Red Cross armband and a small white flag, her dearest friend Julia watched from the doorway of a Moore Street home. [135]

Later, she was arrested with the men and kept outside in the cold and damp without food overnight. The next day she and Carey were transferred to Richmond Barracks while O'Farrell continued to carry surrender orders around to the various rebel positions while in the custody of a British officer. She was kept in custody until May 9, the last of the executions, and then released as a non-combatant.

Later she would work with O'Farrell both as a nurse and a courier during the Irish War of Independence. Both would be anti-Treaty when that agreement was signed in 1921 and would raise funds for the Irish Civil War prisoners. They would remain hostile to the Irish Free State and would also withdraw from the Cumann na mBan when it became apparent to them that the group no longer actively supported their core beliefs. Equally they were disappointed in de Valera's rise to power and his reactionary policies.

O'Farrell and Grenan lived together for more than 30 years in their home on Lower Mount Street. Neither ever married or expressed an interest in other companions and it is generally assumed today that they were lovers but given the prohibitions of the Church and the government's recorded sexism, never publicly acknowl-

[135] "Miss Elizabeth O'Farrell's Story of the Surrender", website of the 1916 Rebellion Museum (http://1916rebellionmuseum.com/1916-easter-rising/elizabeth-ofarrell/, accessed Mar. 16, 2021.)

edged.[136] Grenan died in 1972 and was buried beside O'Farrell who died in 1957. On May 23, 2015, 99 years after they both fought for freedom and equality, Ireland became the first nation to legalize same sex marriage.[137]

ROSIE HACKETT, who helped print the Proclamation and delivered it to James Connolly, was also trained as a medic by Dr. Kathleen Lynn. As a member of the ICA, she saw action at St. Stephen's Green as a courier, and later at the College of Surgeons where she treated the wounded. She was arrested there after the surrender and taken to Dublin Castle, and then imprisoned briefly at the Kilmainham Gaol. When she heard of the death of Conolly, a man she considered both a mentor and a friend, she was devastated. She felt the world had lost a truly noble man, a fighter for social justice, women's suffrage, and worker's rights. She considered the indignity and horror of his death, strapped to a chair as he was riddled with bullets, to be a brutal and senseless murder.

On the first anniversary of Connolly's death, she went with Helena Molony and others to Liberty Hall where they hung a large banner from the roof. In block letters easily read from the street it proclaimed: 'JAMES CONOLLY, MURDERED MAY 12, 1916." The police arrived and tore the banner down. After the police left, they raised the banner again. This time they blocked the front door with a ton of coal so no police could enter, then went up on the roof to guard the banner. It stayed there until 6pm and attracted more than a thousand visitors and passersby. Hackett described what happened next:

Police were mobilized from everywhere, and more than four hundred of them marched across from the Store Street direction and made a square outside Liberty Hall. Thousands of people were watching from

---

[136] Rosemary Rogers, "Wild Irish Women: Elizabeth O'Farrell—A Fearless Woman," *Irish America Magazine,* February/March 2017 (https://irishamerica.com/2017/02/wild-irish-women-elizabeth-ofarrell-a-fearless-woman/, accessed May 15, 2021).
[137] "Same Sex Marriage is Now Legal in the Republic of Ireland," *BBC News,* 15 November 1915 (https://www.bbc.com/news/world-europe-34810598, accessed May 15, 2021).

the Quay on the far side of the river. It took the police a good hour or more before they got in, and the script was there until six in the evening, before they got it down.

I always felt that it was worth it, to see all the trouble the police had in getting it down. No one was arrested.

Of course, if it took four hundred policemen to take four women, what would the newspapers say? We enjoyed it at the time- all the trouble they were put to. They just took the script away and we never heard any more. It was Miss Molony's doings. Historically, Liberty Hall is the most important building that we have in the city. Yet, it is not thought of at all by most people. More things happened there, in connection with the Rising, than in any other place. It really started from there.[138]

In the years that followed, she organized over 70,000 women[139] in the Irish Women's Workers' Union (IWWU) and until her retirement in 1970 ran union shops and labored to improve working conditions for Irish women.

She died in 1976 at the age of 83 after a rich and productive life working to secure basic human rights and dignity for women. She was buried with military honors in Glasnevin Cemetery. In 2014 the Rosie Hackett Bridge crossing the Liffey River[140] was dedicated in her honor. The following year a plaque was unveiled in downtown Dublin commemorating her contributions and that of other women of the Irish Citizen Army who were part of the garrison at St Stephen's Green and the College of Surgeons.

HELENA MOLONY was also seriously affected by the death of James Connolly. When she was in the Kilmainham Gaol she said that she

[138] Statement of Miss Rosie Hackett, Bureau of Military History (Document No. W. S. 546).
[139] Jennifer Gartland, "Rosie Hackett" on the Women's Museum of Ireland website (https://www.womensmuseumofireland.ie/articles/rosie-hackett--2, accessed Oct. 3, 2021).
[140] "Rosie Hackett Bridge" on Bridges of Dublin (http://www.bridgesofdublin.ie/bridges/rosie-hackett-bridge, accessed May 16, 2021).

witnessed him being dragged out, unable to stand, terribly wounded, and then tied to a chair so that he could be shot.

A close friend of Rosie Hackett and a former secretary of IWWU, she was a leader in labor organizing after the Rising. She also joined Hackett in raising the banner on the side of Liberty Hall commemorating the death of James Connolly. Although to some it may have seemed a lark, defying the police and calling it murder, for Molony it was deadly serious. She remembered clearly the horror of that fateful morning in May and said that her life seemed to have come to an end that day.

Fortunately for Ireland and the world, that was not the case. She became the second female president of the Irish Trades Union Congress supporting workers' rights both male and female, until she was forced to retire due to ill health. Unemployed and dependent on friends, she nonetheless continued to work on a volunteer basis for human rights causes including those of women prisoners, and the Peoples Rights Association, a forerunner of Amnesty International. Outspoken and persistent, she became known as "the patron saint of lost causes"[141] as she continued to advocate for those most marginalized in society. She lived with psychiatrist Evelyn O'Brien until her death in 1967. In the conservative Ireland of de Valera, her relationship with another woman and her fierce embracing of unpopular causes led to her being excluded from civic participation.

NELLIE GIFFORD (DONNELLY) was the efficient commissary supervisor operating from the College of Surgeons and supplying comestibles to the other rebel garrisons. She was also aide-de-camp to Countess Markiewicz. She was arrested with Markiewicz and others when Michael Mallin surrendered and was interned in the Kilmainham Gaol. There she was visited by her sister Grace who shortly thereafter married Joseph Plunkett just before his death by firing squad. Grace also converted to Catholicism as did Nellie's other three sisters, all of whom married Catholics. Nellie, however,

---

[141] "Helena Molony, A Revolutionary Life." *History Ireland, Issue 4 (July-August 2013)*, Vol. 21.

a proud republican, was also a staunch Protestant and remained so throughout her life. When most of the women were released from Kilmainham Gaol, she was one of the 12 who continued to be confined to the Mountjoy Prison for a longer term.

Upon her release she travelled to the US where she and other Irish nationalists gave lectures to overflow crowds on the significance of the Rising and raised money for the cause of Irish independence. There she also married Joseph Donnelly and had a daughter, Mauve. However, she and her husband separated a year later, and she returned to Ireland with her daughter.[142]

Back in Ireland she gained some fame as a broadcast journalist and also became an unofficial historian for the independence movement dedicated to preserving records, diaries, photographs, flags and other items. She also organized an exhibition of Easter Rising artifacts and memorabilia for the National Museum of Ireland and subsequently helped coordinate a nation-wide search to collect an impressive body of historic materials related to the Rising, the War of Independence, and the IRA which are an integral part of the museum's collection today.[143]

MARGARET SKINNIDER

Margaret Skinnider was down for the count after being shot three times on Harcourt Street. She was taken to the College of Surgeons until the surrender and then transferred to St. Vincent's Hospital on the other side of St. Stephen's Green. In addition to a bout with pneumonia, she also suffered from painful burns because of the corrosive antiseptic used to treat her wounds. Her parents back in

---

[142] Clare, *Gifford Girls*. Most of the biographical information is distilled from this text.

[143] Brenda Malone, "Material amnesia and the Historical collections of the National Museum of Ireland" (abstract) on the *Making Memory: visual and material cultures of commemoration in Ireland (Dublin, 13-15 Oct. 2016, National Gallery of Ireland and National College of Art and Design* website (https://makingmemoryconference.wordpress.com/abstracts/, accessed May 16, 2021).

Scotland first received a message that she had been killed. Even the man who helped save her life believed she had died after he had left her. Later, her parents received news that she had been paralyzed when one of the bullets struck her spine. It was not until Nora Connolly finally was able to visit her that she was able to write a short note assuring them that she was recovering nicely.[144]

The problem with her recovery, however, was that now a British agent appeared and took her into custody. However, after an investigation by the military during which she refused to answer any questions, the authorities decided that she was a non-combatant and returned her to the hospital to complete her recovery.

Rightly fearing that she would be imprisoned if she lingered in the hospital and her full participation in the Rising was discovered, she left the hospital in the company of visitors. Dressed as a prim school teacher (she was in fact a mathematics teacher in her previous life), the intrepid revolutionary presented herself at Dublin Castle to the military authorities to solicit a travel permit to go back to Glasgow. After a harrowing interview, she was passed on to another officer who, after probing questions, decided she was a non-combatant, and the permit was granted.[145] She went on to Scotland and then to England where she visited some of her former comrades now in Reading Gaol bringing them food, reading material, and smokes.

She returned briefly to Dublin to visit friends and then—fearing imprisonment—fled to the US with the help of de Valera. There she was active in raising funds for the republican cause and visiting former rebels who had sought sanctuary in America. While there she also wrote her exciting account of the Rising and her participation in it alongside Countess Markiewicz and the other women. Even more interesting for her much-neglected personal life, she met Nora O'Keefe, who had been sent by de Valera to assist her in

[144] Skinnider, *op.cit*, Kindle loc.985.
[145] Ibid, loc 1225.

fundraising. They would live harmoniously together until O'Keefe's death in 1961.[146]

When the couple returned to Ireland in late 1917, Skinnider took a position teaching mathematics. During the War of Independence, she was imprisoned by the British Army. In the Irish Civil War, she participated as a courier for the anti-Treaty forces and in 1922 she, like Childers, was arrested on the trumped-up charge of having an illegal weapon and was incarcerated for the remainder of the war and six months beyond.

After her release she applied for a pension from the new Irish government based on her service in the Rising. It was denied without a hearing ostensibly because she was a woman. She then obtained employment as a math teacher in a primary school in Dublin where she worked until her retirement in 1961. She was selected president of the Irish National Teachers' Organization and became well-known as an active campaigner for the rights of women.

When de Valera was elected president, the government finally granted her pension, and she began to receive long overdue recognition for her role in the Rising. The popularity of her book both in the US and abroad may have played a part as the full implications of her story became known. Upon her death in 1971 she was buried next to Countess Markiewicz in Glasnevin Cemetery in Dublin, one of only three women to be buried in the Republican plot.[147] The Irish tricolor covered her coffin and she received military honors. In her book she had written that among the favorite tunes the rebels sang at the encampments throughout Dublin during cold damp nights

[146] Mary McAuliffe, "Margaret Skinnider: radical feminist, militant nationalist, trade union activist", *The Irish Times,* Mar. 16, 2020 (https://www.irishtimes.com/culture/books/margaret-skinnider-radical-feminist-militant-nationalist-trade-union-activist-1.4202266, accessed June 1, 2021).

[147] Tomás Ó Coisdealbha, "Margaret Skinnider (1892-1971)", *Fenian Graves,* Jun. 27, 2016 (https://www.feniangraves.net/Skinnider,%20Margaret/Skinnider%20bio.htm#:~:text=Margaret%20Skinnider%20died%20in%20October%20of%201971.%20She,Dublin%20alongside%20Countess%20Markievicz.%20Contributor%3A%20Tom%C3%A1s%20%C3%93%20Co%C4%B1sdealbha, accessed June 3, 2021).

was a "song of the earlier risings"[148] called "Wrap the Green Flag 'Round me, Boys." It is an appropriate one for her final rest.

> Wrap the green flag 'round me, boys
> To die 'twere far more sweet.
> With Erin's noble emblem, boys,
> To be my winding-sheet
> In life I longed to see it wave,
> And followed where it led,
> But now my eyes grow dim, my hand
> Would grasp its last bright shred.

DR. KATHLEEN LYNN was sent to Kilmainham Gaol along with Markiewicz, Molony and others. Despite the respect of her peers for her heroic work as chief medical officer during the Rising, her parents were not impressed. They felt that she had betrayed her aristocratic background by her involvement in feminist politics and the nationalist cause. They were doubly shamed by her imprisonment. She wrote in her diary that they were

> Oh, so reproachful, they wouldn't listen to me and looked as if they would cast me off forever. How sorry I am for their sorrow. Erin needs very big sacrifices. I am glad they go home tomorrow. Why do they always misunderstand me?[149]

Lynn was kept in jail until early June and then was deported to England. Rather than put her in prison as they did with Markiewicz and others, they assigned her to medical duty with a doctor in Bath. At the end of the year, she was allowed to return to her home in Rathmines and resume her own medical practice.

---

[148] Skinnider, *op.cit.*, loc. 1424.

[149] Kathleen Lynn, May 12, 1916 in "The Revolutionary Diaries of Dr Kathleen Lynn" on the Royal College of Physicians website (https://www.rcpi.ie/heritage-centre/1916-2/revolutionary-diary-kathleen-lynn/, accessed June 3, 2021).

She was elected to the Sinn Fein executive in 1917, although she did not take her seat. In 1919 she established St. Ultan's Children's Hospital with a group of female activists. It was the only hospital in Ireland entirely managed by women. In 1923 she was elected TD[150] of the Sinn Fein but later grew weary of the party's failure to follow through on promises for social reform, health care, and women's rights.

She lived with Madeleine frrench-Mullen as a same-sex couple until Ms. Mullen's death. She always credited the feminist movement with her initial motivation to become involved with the Rising.[151] She saw that as the only way to change the patriarchal structure.

Dr. Lynn died on September 14, 1955. Crowds lined the street as her cortege passed. She was buried in the family plot at Deansgrange Cemetery with full military honors in recognition of her major contributions to the Rising and the War of Independence. Her diaries are preserved in the Archives of the Royal College of Physicians in Ireland.

MADELEINE FFRENCH MULLEN was interned at the Kilmainham Gaol after the Rising and wrote in her diary that she could bear anything as long as "the Doctor" (Kathleen Lynn) was with her.

While they were together along with over 70 other women at the Kilmainham Gaol, she along with Dr. Lynn, Countess Markiewicz and several other "serious offenders" were deported to England. Markiewicz and Mullen were first confined in Mountjoy Prison, while Dr. Lynn was sent to Bath. Later, Markiewicz would be deported to Aylesbury Prison in London. For Mullen, the separation was painful. In addition, the cells were smaller than in Kilmainham, "the door fit like a plug" and let in neither light nor air. When she made a remark on the discomfort one sultry evening, the matron

---

[150] Teachta Dála, abbreviated as TD (plural TDanna in Irish or TDs in English) is a member of Dáil Éireann, the lower house of the Oireachtas (the Irish Parliament). It is the equivalent of terms such as Member of Parliament (MP).

[151] Taillon, op, cit., 30.

"assured me that the cells were not intended for 'ladies.' Of course, if you are not a lady, it doesn't not matter how you suffer from heat..."[152]

She was occasionally cheered by the sight of "Madame" (Markiewicz) when she saw her during the exercise periods: "Poor Madame she wears prison clothes with such an air and the cap is very becoming to her. She also looks so aggressively happy that it makes you ashamed of your grumbling attitude." But then the exercise period ended abruptly for "security reasons," a fear that women might organize a resistance. Overcome by depression without her dear friend, Mullen decided, "I should no longer keep a diary." Her last entry read: "God save Ireland. Thou art not conquered yet thou dear land."[153]

When she finally returned to Ireland, she moved in with Kathleen Lynn at the doctor's home. Together they founded St. Ultan's Children's Hospital which became well-known, not only because it was founded and administered by women but because of its successful treatment of children with congenital diseases and with tuberculosis. Despite opposition from the Catholic Church which considered vaccination "unnatural," thousands of children were saved, and the pair was ultimately able to convince the Irish government to make childhood vaccination a national program.[154] Mullen died at the age of 63 and was mourned by her lifelong friend who outlived her for another 11 years. She was buried in her family plot in Glasnevin Cemetery. In the last years of her life, she spent her time treating children and dropped out of politics completely.

---

[152] Transcript of the Diary of Madeleine ffrench Mullen (http://slinabande.ie/wordpress/wp-content/uploads/2010/01/DiaryMFM1916.pdf, accessed Jun. 3, 2021), 16.
[153] Ibid., 17-18
[154] Jutta Kruse, "Saving Irish national infants, or protecting the Infant nation? Irish Anti-vaccination discourse, 1900-1930" In *History Studies* vol. 13 (https://ulsites.ul.ie/historystudies/sites/default/files/historystudies_13_kruse_national.pdf, accessed Jun. 3, 2021).

NORA CONNOLLY was with her father in his last hours on earth. She describes that meeting on May 11, 1916. He would be shot at dawn.

One night, we were knocked up at about eleven o'clock. There was an ambulance outside the door; and there was a military Captain with it. He said the message he brought to us was: James Connolly was very weak, and wanted to see his wife and eldest daughter. Mama had seen him the day before, and he was very weak; and she half believed him; but I guessed what it was. We were brought in the ambulance up to the Castle. I remember it so well. You know the part of the Castle, where there are a porch and pillars outside; there is a staircase landing above, which branches into corridors; they had soldiers on every step of the staircase; and on the landing they had little mattresses; there were soldiers lying on them; and there were soldiers at every door.

We were brought into the room where Daddy was. He lifted his head, and said: "I suppose you know what this means?" Mama was terribly upset. I remember he said to me - we were talking about various things - he said: "Put your hand under the bedclothes". He slipped some paper into my hand. He said: "Get that out, if you can. It is my last statement". Mama could hardly talk. I remember he said: "Don't cry, Lillie. You will unman me". Mama said: "But your beautiful life, James", she wept. "Hasn't it been a full life? Isn't this a good end?", he said.

Then they took us away; and we got home. We just stood at the window, pulled up the blind, and watched for the dawn; and, after we knew he was gone, the family all came in; and I opened the last statement, and read it.[155]

James Connolly's last statement reads in part as follows:

We went out to break the connection between this country and the British Empire, and to establish an Irish Republic. We believed that the call we then issued to the people of Ireland, was a nobler call, in a holier

[155] Nora Connolly O'Brien's full statement can be read on the Bureau of Military History website (http://www.bureauofmilitaryhistory.ie/reels/...BMH.WSO286. pdf, accessed June 3, 2021).

cause, than any call issued to them during this war, having any connection with the war. We succeeded in proving that Irishmen are ready to die endeavouring (sic) to win for Ireland those national rights which the British Government has been asking them to die to win for Belgium. As long as that remains the case, the cause of Irish Freedom is safe. Believing that the British Government has no right in Ireland, never had any right in Ireland, and never can have any right in Ireland, the presence, in any one generation of Irishmen, of even a respectable minority, ready to die to affirm that truth, makes that Government forever a usurpation and a crime against human progress. I personally thank God that I have lived to see the day when thousands of Irish men and boys, and hundreds of Irish women and girls were ready to affirm that truth, and to attest it with their lives, if need be.
JAMES CONNOLLY, COMMANDANT-GENERAL,
DUBLIN DIVISION
ARMY OF THE IRISH REPUBLIC.[156]

Later, when his wife went to claim his personal effects, an amusing scene took place which indicated the poor state of British intelligence. As Nora relates it.

She told him she had come for her husband's wallet and watch, which had not been handed back. Maxwell sent her to Major Price. He was in Intelligence. Price questioned Mama about her son. "My young son?" He said: "No, I don't mean that son. I mean the other". Mama said: "I have no other son". I was not present at the interview. But she got back the wallet, with her photograph and a few odd papers that were in it. I remembered then I had once got myself into Volunteer uniform; and had a photograph taken; and had signed it, "Your soldier son"; and given it to Daddy. When the wallet was taken, they found the photograph; and they were looking for that son. We never got that photograph back. They were looking for Daddy's "soldier son". Mama said all the questions were about her son, not the boy of fourteen, but the other son.

[156] Ibid.

Fig. 39. Nora Connolly (O'Brien) in 1916 both without and with the Volunteers' uniform. It was the second photo which the British found in Connolly's wallet and which prompted a British Intelligence search for Connolly's supposed son.

MARIE PEROLZ (FLANAGAN) was an actress, a featured performer for the Liberty Players and the National Players and a close friend of Sean Connolly and Helena Molony with whom she often shared billing at the Abbey Theatre. She was also a teacher of Irish language and history and was active in the Irish Women's Workers Union (IWWU). She was a committed socialist and was the registered owner of *Spark*, the socialist newspaper edited by Constance Markiewicz which published many articles by James Connolly. It was perhaps this last connection which incensed the authorities and brought her much undeserved retribution. Connolly and those connected to him seem to be marked for special treatment by the British, almost as if they feared socialism as much as Irish independence.

After the Easter Rising had initially been cancelled, she was instructed by Pearse that it was on again for Easter Monday, and she should get the word to the Volunteers in Cork. She worked as a courier for Pearse until the surrender. She was arrested in Tralee and charged with ownership of "the seditious weekly paper" *Spark*.

She was held in Kilmainham Gaol until June when she was deported to England, first to Aylesbury Prison, and then for an additional term at Lewes Prison.

Such was the unjust and draconian punishment meted out that even the authorities back in London decided to relent after much public outcry. A formal inquiry was held in Parliament which eventually secured her release. Upon her return to Ireland, she was elected acting president of the IWWU until Markiewicz's release from prison.

She later married Joseph Michael Flanagan (known as "Citizen Flanagan"), a fellow socialist and revolutionary. Together they continued to work for both the independence movement and for the rights of labor until her death in 1950.

BRIDGET FOLEY AND NELL RYAN were not considered leaders in the Rising nor were they active combatants. The harshness of their punishments seem inexplicable as both were singled out for deportation to England and incarceration. Bridget Foley did carry messages from the Irish Republican Brotherhood in Dublin to the Cork Brigade. Also, G-Men kept a close watch on her father's typewriter shop on Sackville Street which they suspected was a transfer point for messages and perhaps guns. She had also been doing some typing for Sean McNamara of the IRB in the weeks prior to the Rising. When Easter Monday arrived, she worked as a courier at the GPO. As Easter week progressed and casualties mounted, she opened a first aid station on lower Sackville Street. After the Rising she returned to her family home in Tralee where she was arrested. On May 3 she was taken to Richmond Barracks, then later to Kilmainham Gaol, where she heard the shots of the firing squad. After the executions she was moved to Mountjoy Prison and six weeks later deported to Aylesbury Prison in England.

After her release she became active in providing safe houses for IRA men fleeing the Black and Tans. She worked with the Gaelic League and Cumann na mBan.

28
WOMEN'S RIGHTS:
A FORGOTTEN PROMISE

We believe that the struggle of Ireland for freedom
is a part of the world-wide upward movement.

James Connolly

Although the Proclamation read by Pádraic Pearse at Nelson's Monument on Easter Monday guaranteed equal rights for "Irishmen and Irishwomen," that promise went unfulfilled. The female auxiliary of the Irish Volunteers, Cumann na mBan, were often relegated to domestic chores. The Commander-in-Chief as well as interim president relegated the women under his command to a supporting role and denied them opportunities for combat. Making tea and sandwiches and loading weapons did not put them in harm's way. However, their work as field medics and as couriers taking messages between different commands certainly did, without the benefit of being able to defend themselves with appropriate sidearms. Eamon de Valera, commandant at Boland's Mills, and future president of the Republic, refused to have any women at all in his garrison.

The exception was the Irish Citizen Army led by James Connolly. The most notable women warriors in his group were Margaret Skinnider and Constance Markiewicz, both praised for their courage under fire and their skills. But there were 37 other women combatants in the band of 200 that formed the ICA. In addition, there were many more women among the Volunteers who risked their lives daily in the service of the new republic: nurses, couriers, intermediaries and others. Of all the civilian deaths during the Rising, 53 percent were women, many of whom had no connection to the rebel forces.[157] A sample would include single women such as Margaret Nolan, 26, a factory worker; Bridget Berry, 36, an engine fitter; and young Bridget McKane, 15, on her way to her first job as a box maker. As Hannah Smyth points out in her carefully researched article in *Century Ireland*, most of the married women were identified by their husband's occupation, a pattern which would persist through most of the century. Thus, Catherine David, 59, a barker's wife; Margaret Daley, a bookmaker's wife; Mary Anne Cole, 37, a laborer's wife. Many were shot close to their own homes.

> There was a high concentration of civilian deaths in the Moore Street area given the close proximity to the General Post Office, a focal point of the fights. More specifically, there are examples such as Harriet McCabe of 34 Marlborough Street who was shot at 45 Marlborough Street while out searching for food. Margaret Daley, bootmaker's wife, was shot in her own bedroom at 57 Queen Street; Christian Caffrey, just under 2 years old was killed in her home at 27 Corporation Building, shot while being held in the arms of her mother Sarah Caffrey who worked as a charwoman in four Dublin houses.[158]

So not only did the fighting spirit of the women warriors of Cumann na mBan and the ICA help forge the Republic, but the blood of working women, housewives, mothers, and that of their innocent daughters confirmed the female sacrifice for the cause.

Yet not only was the equal rights promise of the Proclamation delayed until the Free State Constitution of 1922, but even that included restrictions on women serving on juries, and on continuing employment after marriage. The only real victory was the right to

---

[157] Marie Coleman, "How women got involved in the Easter Rising – and why it failed them", *The Conversation*, Apr. 18, 2016, (https://theconversation.com/how-women-got-involved-in-the-easter-rising-and-why-it-failed-them-55771, accessed June 6, 2021).
[158] Hannah Smyth, "The Civilian Dead: Counting the human cost of the 1916 Rising", *RTE.ie: Century Ireland* (http://www.rte.ie/centuryireland/index.php/articles/the-civilian-dead, accessed June 6, 2021).

vote for those over 21. Moreover, the second constitution under the de Valera regime in 1937 was even more restrictive, with prohibitions on reproductive rights, and a clear message that women's role was primarily domestic.

The role of women was set out in the 1937 Constitution in Article 41, titled "The Family." In that Article the family is described as the "natural, primary and fundamental unit group of Society," with the importance of womanhood primarily deriving from "her life within the home" which sustains the "common good of society." Without female domesticity, it argues, society would be made unsustainable and economically unsound. Thus, earlier notifications that "all citizens are equal before the law" was overwritten by the state's endeavor to prevent mothers from needing to "engage in labor to the neglect of their duties in the home."[159] In addition, the Article pre-emptively nullified any law which would enable the "dissolution of marriage," which effectively banned women from petitioning for divorce or to be relieved of being caretakers of the home and family under any circumstances.[160]

Of all the leaders of the Rising, there were only two men who really stood out in support of equal rights for women. Connolly, as noted, enlisted them in the Irish Citizen Army and gave them combat assignments. In addition, it was he who convinced Pearse to include Irish women as equal in rights and privileges in the Proclamation of the new republic. The other leader was Commandant Michael Mallin who was in command at St. Stephen's Green and later at the College of Surgeons. It was he who gave the orders for both Markiewicz and Skinnider to operate as snipers, and later gave the final approval for Skinnider to embark on the dangerous mission of planting explosives. Despite her obvious courage, her poise under fire, her marksmanship, and the overwhelming agreement among her comrades of the significance of her contributions to the

---

[159] Articles 41.2; 41.2.1, and 41.3.2 (1937)
[160] Jared Alves, "Understanding Women's Reactions to the 1937 Irish Constitution", *Jared Alves*, June 17, 2011 (https://jaredalves.com/2011/06/17/understanding-womens-reactions-to-the-1937-irish-constitution/, accessed June 6, 2021).

cause, she was denied a disability pension in the 1920s by the Irish government, because women were not eligible.

LATER VICTORIES CAME WITH A PRICE

On December 18, 1918, Constance Markiewicz became the first woman in history to be elected to the House of Commons, although as a member of Sinn Fein she did not take her seat. From 1919 to 1922 she served in the Irish Dáil as Minister of Labor and became the first female cabinet minister in Ireland and the second in the history of Europe. She left government service in 1922 because of her opposition to elements of the Anglo-Irish Treaty which required an oath of allegiance to the Crown and partition of Ireland. In the subsequent conflict she fought for the Republican cause and after the war toured the US urging support for an inclusive Irish and independent republic. She died on July 16, 1927, at the age of 59 and was refused a state funeral by the Free State government because of her political stance.

WHO WON THE SAN FRANCISCO EARTHQUAKE?

A militaristic US congressman, confident that "might makes right," once asked a woman testifying for peace at a Congressional hearing, "Who won the First World War?" One of his colleagues shouted out, "Who won the San Francisco earthquake?"

A similar response might also apply to the Easter Rising, the Irish War of Independence and the Irish Civil War. A citizenry battered and beleaguered, a capital city bombarded with historic buildings destroyed, a countryside devastated, and women not much better off than when it all began, So, who won? And what exactly did they win? Markiewicz's election was a major step forward for Irish women and showed what could be done; it would be an inspiration to generations of young girls. In addition, by an Act of Parliament, there were changes in 1918 in the electoral system of both Britain and Ireland which gave women over 30 the right to vote with certain property qualifications. By 1928, the right to vote was extended to all women over 21 regardless of property or income.

Still, Ireland remained benightedly conservative. For example, women were exempted from jury duty so that they could remain in the home and attend to domestic duties, depriving them not only of equal rights but also of civic responsibilities. In 1932 the sale and importation of contraceptives was banned. Women were also barred from employment in the Civil Service or any government job after marriage (Marriage Ban of 1935). And in 1937, as previously mentioned, even more restrictions were imposed by the new constitution.[161]

REFERENDUM TO THE RESCUE

But a new generation of young women was becoming active, and they and their children would begin to see ways around the restrictions of a conservative government and its archaic laws and even

[161] *Article 41 The Family*
  1. The State recognises the Family as the natural primary and fundamental unit group of Society, and as a moral institution possessing inalienable and imprescriptible rights, antecedent and superior to all positive law.
  2. The State, therefore, guarantees to protect the Family in its constitution and authority, as the necessary basis of social order and as indispensable to the welfare of the Nation and the State.
  3. In particular, the State recognises that by her life within the home, woman gives to the State a support without which the common good cannot be achieved.
  4. The State shall, therefore, endeavour to ensure that mothers shall not be obliged by economic necessity to engage in labour to the neglect of their duties in the home.
  5. The State pledges itself to guard with special care the institution of Marriage, on which the Family is founded, and to protect it against attack.
  6. No law shall be enacted providing for the grant of a dissolution of marriage.
  7. No person whose marriage has been dissolved under the civil law of any other State but is a subsisting valid marriage under the law for the time being in force within the jurisdiction of the Government and Parliament established by this Constitution shall be capable of contracting a valid marriage within that jurisdiction during the lifetime of the other party to the marriage so dissolved.

the sexist elements of the 1937 Constitution. Unable to get enough liberals elected to change things, they began searching for another method and discovered the little-used but highly effective democratic procedure of referendum. Instead of submitting a proposal to the legislature and having it end up strangled in committee, they would draw up the proposed new law or constitutional amendment and put it on the ballot for a popular vote. Here they had an advantage, since they could publicly advocate for the new law or change, and also urge it privately with their spouses. The second advantage was that in 1973 Ireland was going through a serious recession and needed more women in the workforce. Ireland joined the European Union in that remarkable year and also removed the Marriage Ban for government employment. In 1975 the Equal Pay Directive was signed into law which also prohibited discrimination by gender for promotion and dismissal. In 1992 women were given the right to maternity leave for at least 14 weeks.

In terms of government leadership in 1973, Maire Geoghegan-Quinn became the first female minister since Constance Markiewicz, and has since served in many cabinet posts including that of Minister of Justice, and Minister for Equity and Law Reform. She is currently the head of the European Council for Research and Science. In 1990 Mary Robinson was elected as the first female president of Ireland. In 1997 Mary McAleese followed in her footsteps. It was the first time in the world that two women were elected consecutively as presidents of their country.

In 2015 the Constitution was amended by a national referendum to allow for same-sex marriages. This was the first time that a nation legalized same-sex marriage by a popular vote. In 2018, again by national referendum, the constitution was amended to give women the right to choose abortion.[162]

In the twenty-first century, the referendum has proven to be a critical vehicle for getting around hidebound conservative politicians and expressing the will of the people. It also showed the world

[162] "Irish abortion referendum: Ireland overturns abortion ban", *BBC News*, May 26, 2018 (https://www.bbc.com/news/world-europe-44256152, accessed June 8, 2021).

the importance of political activism and the possibilities of using the vote for something other than the election of traditional party candidates in league with large corporate donors. In this area Irish activists have led the way for the rest of the world.

As thousands of young people each year visit the Women's Museum in Ireland and read the stories of Countess Markiewicz, Dr. Lynn, Nurse Grenan, teacher/warrior Margaret Skinnider and others, it is important to remember that these women came from all walks of life. Some were well-to-do, some members of a profession, some were working women struggling to make ends meet. Some were Protestant, some Catholic. But what they shared was a common bond of solidarity that one hopes will inspire this and coming generations of women in Ireland and abroad. These women were not just out to improve their own lives, grow their own bank accounts, or establish their own reputations. They were out to change society and help lift up those around them. They also recognized the limitation of class as a serious obstacle to equality and sought to remedy that by providing free education to those who were marginalized by being born in less fortunate circumstances.

Thus, the idea of elimination of gender restrictions was closely tied to the elimination of class restrictions through education. Many of the leaders were trained in the professions, but regardless of their disciplines were involved in education. Pearse, although trained as a lawyer, was the founder and headmaster of St. Enda's School and raised funds to support the school as well as liberally spending his own money. Markiewicz, a well-to-do matron, sold her jewelry to feed the poor, and taught Irish literature and language in her spare time. Skinnider was a mathematics teacher, as was de Valera. Thomas Ashe, leader of the Fingal Volunteers. influenced by family stories of hunger, eviction, and injustice, was an ardent socialist and imbued his followers with ideals of social justice. The irrepressible Dr. Lynn was not only an able physician, but also trained young nurses and established her own hospital to treat the needy.

They all understood that inequality was fundamentally tied to class distinctions which dictated much of one's life from birth. The only way to eliminate those distinctions, and truly achieve the feminist goal of equal opportunities for all regardless of gender, was to educate those born to less fortunate circumstances and to use the collective wealth of the state to do that.

Believing that, as the poet wrote, "It is not what we give but what we share/For the gift without the giver is bare,"[163] they saw that leadership demanded that they contribute a portion of their own time, energy, and expertise in volunteer work to achieve this goal. They considered public service a requisite of true citizenship and one of the essential underpinnings of true feminism.

---

163 James Russell Lowell, "The Vision of Sir Launfal."

29

THE DECEPTIVE NATURE OF FREEDOM

When questions of 'class' interests are eliminated
from public controversy a victory is thereby gained
for the possessing, conservative class, whose only
hope of security lies in such elimination.

James Connolly, *Labour in Irish History*

When the Casement Report on the Congo was published and the world discovered the horrors of King Leopold II's crimes, control of the region was passed from his elite group of cronies to the more liberal Belgium Congress. It was assumed that now the workers of that beleaguered country would be treated humanely and that they would be freed of the shackles of forced labor. Unfortunately, it was not to be the case. The Congress, unable to manage the complexities of the region, nor recover the costs of their purchase from Leopold, sold concessions to corporations that continued to drain the country's resources and bind the people to a wage serfdom. The revolution which followed provided a brief interlude in which the country moved toward a socialist goal, but this was interrupted by Western powers claiming it was a communist conspiracy and setting up a puppet government which provided business as usual for the corporations involved in extracting the Congo's resources for profit.

So, when James Connolly wrote in Ireland about the danger of simply exchanging one master for another, he was clearly a harbinger of the future. His warning bearing repeating:

If you remove the English Army tomorrow and hoist the green flag over Dublin Castle, unless you set about the organization of the Socialist Republic your efforts will be in vain. England will still rule you. She would rule you through her capitalists, through her landlords, through her financiers, through the whole array of commercial and individualist institutions she has planted in this country and watered with the tears of our mothers and the blood of our martyrs.[164]

A whole array of commercial institutions now rule the world. Politicians are simply puppets whose strings they pull. Those corporate entities which are defined as "persons" under corporate law so that they have limited liability also contribute vast amounts to elected politicians. They determine which crops will be planted in a country, which natural resources will be extracted, and which concessions must be made by the government. They enforce their will through arbitration agreements which ensure that the stockholders and CEOs profit and, as John D. Rockefeller once said, "The public be damned!" By relocating their facilities at will, they determine which pollution laws they will obey, which taxes they will pay, and who will work for them and for how much. They undermine workers' unions, thus inducing "mobility of labor." In some cases, they eliminate the employee relationship entirely by accepting only consultancy contracts (the Uber model now followed by many corporations and governments), thus avoiding liability, eliminating employer tax payments, insurance coverage, social security contributions, and retirement packages.

Connolly wrote that "governments in capitalist society are but committees of the rich to manage the affairs of the capitalist class."[165] He was very close to the twenty-first century equivalent. Governments today are representatives of the corporations who have been chosen to facilitate business concerns. And when they fail to do so, the corporate attorneys invoke the special agreements

---

[164] Beresford Ellis (ed.), 124.
[165] Ibid., 248.

for TNC arbitration[166] in which the interests of the corporate entity and its shareholders are usually convincingly presented by a team of lawyers to the detriment of the state and the people who unbeknownst to themselves are on the road to peonage and neofeudalism.[167] Called Investor State Dispute Settlements (ISDS), such agreements might be new to Ireland, but have become quite common in Latin America. Governments of all political stripes have faced multi-million (sometimes billion) dollar arbitration cases resulting in court rulings conforming to the interests of multinational corporations, especially mining and other extractive companies. [168]

WAS THE RISING REALLY ABOUT SOCIALISM?

Some historians have suggested that social injustice was not a significant issue for most of the leadership of the Rising. Historian John Dorney reminds us that the Easter Rising differed from previous revolts in which the nationalists supported ordinary folks in the countryside who wished to wrest their land from the mostly Anglo-Irish landed class.

> Since the 1903 Wyndham Act, Irish tenants had bought the land with British government loans...Whereas in 1870 97% of the land was owned by landlords and 50% by just 750 families, in 1916 70% of Irish families owned their own land. The Irish export trade in cattle and daily

[166] Transnational Corporation Agreements. See "Transnational Corporations: What Regulations?", *Stop Corporate Impunity* (https://www.stopcorporateimpunity.org/transnational-corporations-what-regulations/, accessed June 7, 2021).

[167] Michael Hudson, "The Road to Debt Deflation, Debt Peonage, and Neofeudalism", Levy Economics Institute of Bard College website, February 2012 (http://www.levyinstitute.org/publications/the-road-to-debt-deflation-debt-peonage-and-neofeudalism, accessed June 7, 2021).

[168] "Investor-State Dispute Settlement in Latin America", Georgetown Law website (https://www.law.georgetown.edu/carola/news-events/2019-2020-events/isds-in-latin-america/, accessed June 7, 2021).

products was also booming and much of rural Ireland had never been better off. [169]

But the 70 percent of the land these Irish families owned were largely small plots that in many cases produced little more than subsistence. Landlords still held most of the large tracts of acreage throughout the country, and cattle grazers had replaced tenant farmers. Moreover, the loans from British banks, for 70 years at 3 percent interest, placed the small "landowners" (and their heirs, unless they sold the land, as most eventually did) in the shackles of debt peonage. Meanwhile in the cities, as the Dublin lockout of 1913 clearly demonstrated, the owners of industry were in league with the forces of repression to see that significant change was not to be forthcoming but rather compromised as small wage increments or prestige positions were given to malleable workers.

Moreover, these concessions were intended to keep the flock of Irish peasants pacified by being admitted to the "landowning class," or by promoting certain workers to middle management as foremen or supervisors along with a raise in pay. These were the stratagems employed to encourage the working class and peasantry to believe that they too were, or could be, a part of the new ruling class. It is an attitude which has persisted to this day, not only in Ireland, but in the US and other countries as well. The belief that if you are the owner of your house and a piece of land, you are middle class and one of those who have a voice in how your country is run. It is a dangerous illusion. As an editorial note in a newspaper of the day warned, "Compromise has eaten like a cancer into our political life."

Connolly's warning of the failure of systematic change still stands as a prophecy when he wrote, "the green-coated Irish soldiers will guard the fraudulent gains of capitalist and landlord from 'the thin

---

[169] John Dorney, "Slaves or Freemen: Sean McDermott and the psychology of the Easter Rising" (https://www.academia.edu/729540/Slaves_or_Freemen_Sean_McDermott_the_IRB_and_the_psychology_of_the_Easter_Rising?email_work_card=title, PDF, accessed June 7, 2021).

hands of the poor' just as remorselessly and just as effectually as the scarlet-coated emissaries of England do today."[170]

And for those who see compromise and using feminist gains or political insider knowledge to procure corporate largess or advantage, or those young girls who see their ultimate victory as being a CEO, or the young politicians or military officers who look for profitable consultancies or lobbyist positions at the end of their tenure, it is wise to keep the admonition of John F. Kennedy in mind: Throughout history, "those who foolishly sought power by riding the back of the tiger ended up inside."

When the "Celtic Tiger"[171] was touted as the new economic direction of Ireland and recession fears faded, many rushed to fill the new corporate management ranks, and several of these began to open up to women. It seemed like the natural progression for the feminist movement. However, like many dreams of wealth fostered by global investment and corporate outreach, it claimed many more victims in its maw. But since the financial news and even university brochures are produced by corporate media and public relations firms, the focus has not been on what has been lost by many, the evictions, the downsizing, the redundancies, and forced emigration of youth, but rather on the gains that have been made by the few lucky ones.

The "news" outlets carry stories daily of such successes among women in Ireland. To cite one example, a recent news item touts the success of women leaders of ISEQ-listed corporations. The ISEQ in Ireland lists those companies with the highest trading volume and the best performance. It includes major banks, insurance companies, real estate enterprises and media giants. Ireland's top 20 ISEQ corporations, according to this report, have the largest

---

[170] James Connolly, "Socialism and Nationalism", 1897, *Marxists.org* (https://www.marxists.org/archive/connolly/1897/01/socnat.htm, accessed June 7, 2021).

[171] Celtic Tiger " (Irish: An Tíogar Ceilteach) is a term referring to the economy of the Republic of Ireland from the mid-1990s to the late 2000s, a period of rapid real economic growth fueled by foreign direct investment. The boom was dampened by a subsequent property bubble which resulted in a severe economic downturn.

ratio of female CEOs globally. They include Bank of Ireland's head, Francesca McDonagh; the CEO of Gambia, Siobhan Talbot; and Irish Rental Properties' CEO, Margaret Sweeney.[172]

Ireland, according to the news release, can claim 15 percent of women in the highest managerial positions, compared to Denmark's 13 percent, Norway's 12 percent, and a global average of 5 percent. Many see this not only as a benchmark but also as significant under-representation of women and wish to propel even more into these positions of power, as if that is the end goal of feminist achievement.

WHAT IS WRONG WITH THIS GOAL?

While economic empowerment is a legitimate goal and those who rise to the top of their profession deserve respect, it is clear that this capitalist benchmark falls far short of the fundamental change which feminists fought for, went to prison for, and often risked their lives for.

A more sustainable position is what is called "intersectional feminism"[173], which is more in line with what Connolly theorized and Dr. Lynn and her fellow feminists put into practice. It was the realization that there are many "feminisms" differentiated by class, by race, by economic exploitation, by privilege. Many women have limited opportunities not because of lack of motivation, or even in some cases lack of skills, but rather because the social conditions they live in limit their opportunities.

The success of a handful of female CEOs, much like basketball players in the NBA, is that of a chosen few who have the natural

---

[172] Joe Brennan, "Ireland's top ISEQ companies have the highest ratio of female CEOs globally", *Irish Times*, Nov. 23, 2020 (https://www.usatoday.com/story/news/2017/01/19/feminism-intersectionality-racism-sexism-class/96633750/, accessed June 8, 2021).

[173] Alia E. Dastagir, "What is intersectional feminism? A look at the term you may be hearing a lot", *USA Today* (https://www.usatoday.com/story/news/2017/01/19/feminism-intersectionality-racism-sexism-class/96633750/, accessed June 8, 2021).

abilities or birthright connections, as well the skills and the opportunities to rise to those positions. They are exceptions. Their success does nothing to diminish the inequities which are systemic and, in many cases, may even help to legitimize them. As Marija Asseveckova, a young feminist scholar, explains:

> The intersectional feminist seeks to unveil the roots of discrimination in economies, ideologies and distributions of power. For intersectional feminists, gender is not the only issue; race, class, age, ethnicity and education matter as well. All these characteristics can make a woman more or less privileged in comparison to her fellow citizens. Making women's success pivotal might be a dangerous thing – the slippery slope of identity politics is that we might praise economically empowered women who are as invested in maintaining the status quo of inequality and exploitation as men.[174]

The intersectional feminists argue convincingly that we should all join in the struggle not only to eliminate gender inequality but also the inequalities between more and less privileged women. The latter face such challenges as violence, whether domestic or institutionalized, cultural conservatism, religious restrictions, crippling poverty, malnutrition, and lack of educational resources. The goals of the true feminist coincide with those of the committed socialist, understanding that they must be multidimensional, and while the efforts should begin locally, they must extend global when resources permit. As Asseveckova reminds us:

> There is little doubt that feminism must discuss economic issues; if topics such as precarious employment opportunities, the wage gap, student debts and a volatile financial future are excluded from feminist debates,

[174] Marija Asseveckova, "Women and the Economy: Why women becoming CEOs man=y not be the best benchmark for feminism", *Young Feminists,* Jan. 31, 2016 (https://www.youngfeminist.eu/2016/01/women-and-the-economy-why-women-becoming-ceos-might-not-be-the-best-benchmark-for-feminism/, accessed June 8, 2021).

the whole movement would become estranged from reality. However, it would be better if feminists questioned the very concept of economic success in a divided world full of exploitation and inequality. Economic empowerment does not necessarily mean becoming a member of the ruling class. Indisputably praising those women who managed to get through the glass ceilings and gender stereotypes and become a top-manager is a one-dimensional response to limited economic empowerment. Behind every CEO, male or female, there are thousands of people who could be made redundant or exposed to unbearable working conditions by that person. To give voice to people who are less privileged should be vital for any social movement if it claims to promote equality; women all over the world are at a heightened risk for poverty... Therefore, an intersectional form of feminism which takes into account not only gender, but class is the way forward.[175]

Without economic freedom, social mobility comes to a standstill.[176] Without education, access to healthy air, safe streets in a secure homeland, fresh water, and nutritious food, there is no real freedom, and equality of opportunity is mere rhetoric.

[175] Ibid.
[176] See Michael Elbrecht, "An Inquiry Into the Relationship Between Economic Freedom and Social Mobility," *Thesis. Florida State University.*

30
HISTORIOGRAPHY

S omc people think that the professional historians' personal commitments — to their people, their country, their religion, their language — undermine their professional objectivity. Not so. Not so, as long as historians respect the integrity of their sources and adhere strictly to the principles of sound scholarship. Personal commitments do not distort, but instead they enrich historical writing. — Lucy Dawidowicz, author of *The Holocaust and the Historians* (1981)

The feminist historian Ruth Taillon correctly notes that the women of 1916 were passionately involved with what Constance Markiewicz called "the three great movements of the time." These were land reform, women's rights, and urban worker's rights. She goes on to add a fourth: participation in the cultural revival through participation in the Gaelic League and related social activities that included music, dance, Irish language classes, and poetry readings.[177] I would agree but suggest that this was just the beginning and that these elements, coupled with those outlined below, are part of a larger and more complete picture.

Socialism was a major strand of the new mentality which resulted in the Rising. While it was derived from land reform and urban worker movements, it grew into something greater through the international sharing of its philosophical underpinnings via books, magazine articles and lectures. A new realization dawned on many who had previously not given it much thought. They came to believe that the resources of a country should belong to the people

---

[177] Ruth Taillon, *The Women of 1916*. Second edition. (Dublin: Tara Press, 2018), 30.

of that country and that these resources should be accessible to all. This fit perfectly with...

Nationalism, the belief that no outside force, whether corporate or imperial, should determine the welfare of the inhabitants, or prevent the equitable distribution of national resources. And with that understanding came a sense of patriotism which was shared through...

Symbolism, the imaginative ability of a people to define their shared beliefs with representational images and colors that illustrated their commonalities, their historical past, and their hopes for the future. These were also outward signs of a shared...

Spirituality because these symbols were not neutral but represented deep feelings and common connections. It was no accident that "The Rising" was the chosen name for the insurrection or that it occurred during Easter week. "Though you may die, you will live forever." Christ's death was symbolic, not merely of Christ but of all sacrifices which bring about victory, all self-abnegations which bring about spiritual renewal. As St. Paul reminded the Romans, "I live; yet not I, but Christ liveth in me." Even *green,* the color of springtime, of new birth, of renewal, pointed to the promise of fruitful bounty. And with the spiritual rebirth would come a...

Cultural renewal symbolized by the harp, representing a culture that predated the foreign invasions and had existed, as Cornelius McGillicuddy once famously said, "when the Anglo-Saxons were still swinging by the tails from trees." This re-elevation of the Irish language, Irish poetry and music to a position of cultural importance was also an integral part of the Rising and its effects echo though the world today "wherever green is worn," in the words of the Irish poet. The word "revolution" itself means not merely an overthrow of what currently exists, but a return to something that existed before when the "common wealth" of the nation was something shared, and the "gift economy"[178], as described by the poet Sam Hammill, was a reality.

The full meaning of the Rising and the role of women was (and is today) only imperfectly understood. Each generation of historians hopes to add its own bit of understanding as the contrasting and complimenting threads of the past are unraveled and then woven back together. But one thing is clear: the men and women of the Rising who shared some, but not all of these ideas and passions, were nonetheless committed to the Cause, and it was this solidarity which brought them together, not as a collective, but as individuals with their own skills, faiths, and family backgrounds, willing to submerge idiosyncrasies and differences in support of the larger cause. Not all were feminists, or socialists, or even considered learning the Irish language a priority. As Louise Gaven Duffy, the irrepressible secretary of Cumann na mBan, wrote:

> There were those who didn't share those opinions, but the affairs of the Volunteers were so important and so necessary that we couldn't afford to divide our energies and our responsibilities. We put every other consideration aside and were ready to do what we were asked to do. [179]

She herself felt that the Rising was precipitous, and was not in agreement, but as she noted in her diary on Easter Monday at the GPO:

---

[178] Sam Hamill, "Shadow Work," *American Poetry Review*, Vol.15, No.6, Nov/Dec 1986, 5-7. The term refers to all that work which is not compensated by monetary exchange or by barter. Hamill notes that much of what we truly value in life, chores and activities which make out homes livable, our interactions seamless, our daily lives less perilous, consist of tasks for which we are not really compensated. The policeman who goes out of his way to give directions, the motorist who stops to assist with a flat tyre, the neighbor who lends his saw to cut a broken tree limb, the teacher who spends her free time with a troubled student, the spontaneous compliment, the helping hand to a workmate, and almost all of what has been derogatorily labeled "women's work" in the household.

[179] Louise Gavan Duffy, *In the GPO: Cumann na mBan*, translated by J. Jackson, quoted in Taillon, *op.cit.* 32-33.

I was brought to Pearse and had the temerity to tell him that I thought the rebellion was very wrong as it would certainly fail but that I wished to be there if there was going to be anything doing.[180]

That statement speaks volumes. Knowing that it was ill conceived (given the lack of arms and the minimal assistance from outside Dublin), knowing that it would certainly fail in the immediate and practical sense, she went ahead anyway. It is clear from the statements made by Irish rebels both during and after the Rising that the traditional concepts of victory and success were never indispensable to what the Rising was about. Pearse felt that if they lasted four days and were to be seen as combatants in the international sense, it would be a success. Armed with mostly outdated rifles, facing a force 15 times larger, they outfought soldiers armed with artillery and machine guns for almost an entire week. Many of the leaders, including Markiewicz, felt that being sentenced to death was a victory because it showed the desperate measures to which the British had been driven by the Irish determination to be free. They believed that the rest of the civilized world would condemn the Empire and rally behind the Irish. They were not wholly mistaken.

BLOOD SACRIFICE

Lauren Oyler, the American critic, wrote that "We live in a time where past concepts of an order larger than the self are dwindling away or have disappeared."[181] As a result it is sometimes difficult for a contemporary westerner to understand blood sacrifice as a concept other than that espoused by suicidal bombers and terrorists. And yet firefighters and police, health care workers, warriors in the UN Peacekeeping Forces, and healers in Doctors Without Borders,

---

[180] Louise Gavan Duffy's Statement By Witness Document *Bureau of Military History* (http://goo.gl/JkybME, accessed June 8, 2021).
[181] Lauren Oyler, "Le Mot Juste," *Harpers Archive*, Oct. 2020 (https://harpers.org/archive/2020/10/le-mot-juste-collected-stories-shirley-hazzard/, accessed June 8, 2021).

risk their lives daily to keep people safe, not merely in their own communities but around the world.

Irish history has several examples of those who sacrificed their lives for the freedom of their beleaguered island, among them Wolfe Tone and Robert Emmet. But by 1914, many moderates were convinced that the Home Rule bill was a fair compromise and encouraged young Irish boys to serve in the British Army as true subjects of Her Majesty when the war broke out.

It was apparent to the Irish Republican Brotherhood that Ireland would forever be enslaved by its Imperial neighbor if that portion of populace which had grown complaisant and resigned to the status quo continued to grow and prosper. As more and more people accepted as "normal" small daily humiliations and national subjugation, they would lose the will to resist; they would be a downtrodden and lost people, whose very own culture and language would be lost and absorbed in the Empire where they were mere "subjects" rather than citizens. As Séan MacDermott, one of the most influential leaders of the IRB, noted two years before the Rising:

> The Irish patriot spirit will die forever unless a blood sacrifice is made in the next few years. It will be necessary for some of us to offer ourselves as martyrs if nothing better can revive the national Irish spirit.[182]

MacDermott's decision to go ahead with the Rising even though he knew they had insufficient men and ammunition to have a significant chance of success may seem foolhardy. Indeed, John Dorney explores that very point in his seminal article on the psychology of blood sacrifice.

> So we are left with a puzzling question. We have a highly capable, brave and psychologically strong activist, who organised and helped to lead a Rising he knew did not have mass support and which he must have known could not succeed militarily. He was thrown into the deepest

---

[182] Fallon, "Putting the language of Pearse in content"; see note 110. .

depression when faced with the prospect that it would not come off and declared that he had never been happier than when facing his own execution as a consequence.[183]

MacDermott's speech in 1914 calling for a blood sacrifice echoes that of Patrick Henry in the House of Burgesses in Virginia and does not seem extreme to Americans given the context. Yet, the subjection of humiliation, indeed the needless deaths suffered by the Irish in the 1840 during the Great Hunger when England was exporting foodstuffs from Ireland, outstrip any hardships ever suffered by the American colonists who were more than willing to commit their lives, their fortunes and their sacred honor to fight that same Empire. As Patrick Henry expressed it in the Virginia House of Burgesses in 1775:

> Is life so dear, or peace so sweet, as to be purchased at the price of chains and slavery? Forbid it, Almighty God! I know not what course others may take; but as for me, give me liberty, or give me death![184]

After the surrender, as the Volunteers were being marched into captivity, MacDermott told a fellow captive, "The cause is lost if we are not shot." His companion replied, "Surely you don't mean that, Séan. Aren't things bad enough?" MacDermott grimly replied, "They are so bad that if what I say does not come true, they will be very much worse."[185]

Finally, after he was convicted and sentenced to death, he wrote a letter home which said in part, "I feel happiness the likes of which I have never experienced. I die that the Irish nation might live."[186]

---

[183] Dorney, "Slaves or freemen"; see note 166. .
[184] Patrick Henry, "Patrick Henry's Speech Before the Virginia House of Burgesses, Richmond, Virginia March 23,1775", *Lit2Go* (https://etc.usf.edu/lit2go/133/historic-american-documents/4956/patrick-henrys-speech-to-the-virginia-house-of-burgesses-richmond-virginia-march-23-1775/, accessed June 10, 2021).
[185] https://www.theirishstory.com/2011/04/23/%E2%80%98slaves-or-freemen%E2%80%99-sean-mcdermott-the-irb-and-the-psychology-of-the-easter-rising/#.YWW1G9rMKUk
[186] Ibid.

So, for MacDermott, the gift of his life made perfect sense. He had made the sacrifice so that future generations would be free. He had stepped forward so that his descendants would be able to make rational choices, not ones based on fear or dictated by a foreign power. In addition, by surrendering in a timely fashion, he ensured that only the nominal leadership would be called to die, and there would be no more civilian or military casualties. A large number of the insurgents felt the same way and acted out of their beliefs with great courage. Countess Markiewicz, when told by the military tribunal that her death sentence had been commuted, reportedly said, "I do wish that your lot had the decency to shoot me."[187]

For these men and women words like "duty" and "service" did not ring hollow as they do to many cynical contemporary ears. They served a cause higher than themselves and had the courage to see it through to their deaths even though they couldn't know the final results of their efforts. Martin Luther King, who also knew about committing to fight against overwhelming odds, once wrote that courage was the root of all virtues. Without it, one eventually retreats from one's principles and makes compromises.

For those 77 women who went to prison as a result of their activities, it is important to note the solidarity, the *esprit de corps* and the general good humor with which they approached the deprivation and hardship. Far from being cowed or intimidated by soldiers who led them into captivity, they went with their heads held high. Most notable among them was Rose Pat McNamara.

She was a quartermaster and supervisor of nurses and at the time of the surrender she was at the Marrowbone Lane Garrison based in the Jameson Distillery. It was one of the last garrisons to surrender. Because she appeared to be a non-combatant, they offered her and 22 other women the opportunity to walk away and return to their homes. She refused. She and the other women then marched out

---

[187] "1916: Not Constance Markiewicz, 'I do wish your lot had the decency to shoot me'", *ExecutedToday.com,* May 6, 2018 (https://www.executedtoday.com/2018/05/06/1916-not-constance-markievicz-i-do-wish-your-lot-had-the-decency-to-shoot-me/, accessed Oct. 4, 2021).

Fig. 40. Rose Pat McNamara.

with the men off to prison. On the way they sang a ditty that was a favorite of Constance Markiewicz, called "The Felons of Our Land."

> Let coward sneer and tyrant frown
> Oh, little do we care.
> The felon's cap's the noblest crown
> An Irish head can wear.
> And every Gael in Innisfail
> Who scorns the serf's vile brand
> From Lee to Boyne would gladly join
> The felons of our land.

It is a song that encapsulates the decisions that many principled individuals have made throughout history: Mahatma Gandhi, Martin Luther King, Emmeline Pankhurst, Henry David Thoreau, Nelson Mandela, and Lucy Burns among many, many others. Thoreau, who went to prison rather than pay taxes to support an unjust war when the US invaded Mexico, was asked by his friend Emerson what on earth he was doing in prison. Thoreau reportedly replied, "What are you doing out of prison? It is where any true American should be." Lucy Burns and other suffragists[188] were imprisoned, some were even chained to the floors of their cells for refusing to end their protest for the right to vote and return to their homes. During her trial in 1908 Emmeline Pankhurst told the court: "We are here not because we are law-breakers; we are here in our efforts to become law-makers."[189]

Fig. 41. The arrest of Emmeline Parkhurst during a suffrage march in London. May 1914 at Kingsgate.

ENVOI

Historiography is the writing of history based on the critical examination of sources, the selection of particular details from the authentic materials in those sources, and the synthesis of those details into a narrative that stands the test of critical examination. When we look at the history of the Rising, we see that it was defined

---

[188] Some readers might be more familiar with the term "suffragette." This was coined by a British journalist in 1908 as a disparaging term. The correct word is suffragist.

[189] Paula Bartley, *Emmeline Pankhurst* (London: Routledge, 2003), 129-130.

by certain clear characteristics which were not incidental but were intrinsic to the uprising.

The first encompassed land reform, workers' rights movements, union building and strikes, all of which came to a head in the late nineteenth and early twentieth centuries in the cauldron of an oppressed colonial nation. Most of the major leaders were in some way or another committed to a portion of the social vision whether in support of the Dublin lockout, economic relief for the needy, or universal health care. Many historians have been reluctant to affirm these aspects lest they be branded as Marxists and result in their books being rejected by traditional publishing houses and excluded from lucrative research grants.

The second concerned equal rights and opportunities for women coupled with equal obligations and risks. This characteristic was very much a part of the Rising. And it was not a quality affirmed solely by women only but one shared with major male leaders like Connolly. These feminists were not looking for a chance to be the next CEO of a major corporation but rather to lead the fight against the dominance of corporate interests over their society. They were not looking for special privileges but rather the opportunity to serve alongside the men in a variety of roles not limited by gender prejudice. Too many today carry the gender or race sword of retributive justice to carve out their own piece of the corporate pie. Others see feminist theory as a way of replacing the paternalism with their own feminist version thus reinforcing the pyramid instead of seeing institutionalized plutocracy as the instigator and promoter of divisiveness, racism, and misogyny, and turning the pyramid upside down or eliminating it altogether.

Finally, service, self-sacrifice, as well as spiritual and cultural renewal were part of the Rising. These rebels did not want the Rising to result in a replacement of one flag with another, one dominant class with another, one rapacious culture with another. They looked to build a community of citizens who were willing to sacrifice for the good of the whole, willing to contribute to the gift economy, willing to give instead of take. They looked for not only a rebirth of freedom but a rebirth of culture, language, song, poetry and feeling of belonging to something larger than the self, larger even that mere nationalism or any inflexible ideology. They looked for a new humanism that all would have a share in. That is the true message of the Rising. This is the message that would reach from the plough to the stars, that would inspire the world. It is not an imagined vision by this historian but one which was imperfectly but sincerely envisioned by those who gave their lives so that this new society would arise falteringly, sometimes painfully, but ultimately triumphant.

BIBLIOGRAPHY

I. MISCELLANEOUS SOURCES AND ARCHIVES

An Chartlann Náisúnta. The National Archives of Ireland. (Dublin, Ireland).

Archive of Sinn Fein Documents.

Boston College Library (Chestnut Hill, USA).

Burner Library Collection: Irish and Irish American.

British Library, Newspaper Library Archives 1912-1916.

Bureau of Military History
Witness statements (oral histories from participants of the Rising of 1916).

Hay Library Special Collections.

Brown University (Providence, USA).

Georgetown Law Library (Washington, DC).

Hesburgh Library, University of Notre Dame (South Bend, USA).
(a)Digital Exhibits and Collections.
(b)The Irish Rebellion and People in 1916.
(c)Hesburgh Special Collections.

Institute of Historical Research.

Irish History Collection.

School of Advanced Study, London.

Irish American Heritage Center (Chicago, USA).

Irish American Cultural Center (New York, USA).

Irish Studies Archives

University of Notre Dame

National University of Ireland (Galway).

Public Records Office of Northern Ireland (PRONI).

The National Library of Ireland (Dublin, Ireland).
  (a)National Photographic Archive.
  (b)Waking the Feminists Digital Archive.
  (c) Genealogical Office.
Swarthmore College Peace Collection (Swarthmore, PA).
The Queen's Library of Belfast.
Trinity College Library (Dublin, Ireland).
Villanova University Library.
  (a) Home Before the Leaves Fall: A Great War Centennial Exhibition.
  (b) Mail Call: News and Letters from the Great War.

II. NEWSPAPERS AND JOURNALS

Atlanta Constitution
Daily Mirror (London)
History Ireland
IRIS Magazine
Irish American Magazine.
Irish Newspaper Archives On-line
Saoirse Irish Freedom
The Brandsma Review
The Echo
The Irish Examiner
The Irish News
The Kerryman
The Irish Humanist
The Irish Times (Sinn Fein Rebellion Handbook 1917)
Limerick Leader

III. BOOKS AND ARTICLES

Arrington, Lauren. *Revolutionary Lives: Constance and Casimir Markiewicz.* Princeton: Princeton University Press, 2016.

Bartley, Paula. *Emmeline Pankhurst.* London: Routledge, 2003.

Bouch, J.J. "Republican Proclamation of 1916." *Bibliographical Society of Ireland,* vol. V (1933-38), no. 3.

Clare, Anne. *Unlikely Rebels: The Gifford Girls and the Fight for Irish Freedom.* Dublin: Mercier Press, 2011.

Coffey, Thomas M. *Agony at Easter: The 1916 Uprising.* New York: Penguin 1971.

Conlon, Lil. "Cumann na mBan and the Women of Ireland. 1913-1925." Kilkenny: *Kilkenny People,* 1916. Wordpress.com Archives, 1969.

Connolly, Linda. *Women and the Irish Revolution: Feminism, Activism, Violence.* Dublin: Irish Academic Press, 2020.

Coogan, Tim Pat. *Michael Collins, A Biography.* London: Arrow Books, Ltd., 1991.

Caulfield, Max. *The Easter Rebellion.* Dublin: Gill Books. Kindle ed., 2010.

DeRosa, Peter. *Rebels: The Irish Rising of 1916.* New York: Ballantine Books, 1992.

Dorney, John. "The Easter Rising in County Wexford." *The Irish Story,* 10 April 2012.

_____ "The Easter Rising in County Galway." *The Irish Story,* 4 March 2016.

Edwards, Owen Dudley, and F. Pyle. *1916: The Easter Rising.* London: MacGibbon & Kee, 1968.

Ellis, Peter Beresford, ed. *James Connolly - Selected Writings.* London: Pluto Press, 1988.

Flint, Colin, ed. *The Geography of War and Peace: From Death Camps to Diplomacy.* New York: Oxford University Press, 2005.

Flannery, James W. *W.B.Yeats and the Idea of a Theatre.* New Haven: Yale University Press, 1976.

Lynch, Diarmuid (author) and O'Donoghue, Florence (editor). *The IRB and the 1916 Rising.* Cork: Mercier, 1957.

Frawley, Oona. *Women and the Decade of Commemoration (Irish Culture, Memory, Place).* Bloomington: Illinois University Press, 2021.

Hammill, Sam. "Shadow Work" in *The American Poetry Review.* Vol. 15, No. 6. Nov/Dec 1986, 5-7.

Hay, Carol. *Think Like A Feminist.* New York: W.W.Norton & Co., 2020.

Hochschild, Adam. *King Leopold's Ghost: A Story of Greed, Terror and Heroism in Colonial Africa.* New York: Mariner Books, 1999.

Hogan, Michael. *The Irish Soldiers of Mexico.* Guadalajara: Fondo Editorial Universitario, 1997.

Macardle, Dorothy, *The Irish Republic.* Internet Archives: Corgi Books, 1968.

Macartney, Donal. "Gaelic Ideological Origins of 1916," in Owen Dudley Edwards and F. Pyle, eds., *1916: The Easter Rising.* London: MacGibbon & Kee, 1968.

MacLochlainn, Piaras F. *Last Words, Letters And Statements Of The Leaders Executed After The Rising of Easter, 1916.* Dublin: Kilmainham Jail Restoration Society, 1971.

Martin, F.X. "1916—Myth, Fact and Mystery" in *Studia Hibernica,* 7, (1967), 7-126.

_____ *The Howth Gun-Running and the Kilcoole Gun-Running. Forward by Eamon de Valera.* Newbridge, Kildare: Marion, 2014.

Matthews, Ann. *Renegades: Irish Republican Women 1910-1922.* Dublin: Mercier Press, 2010.

McAuliffe, Bridget, McAuliffe, Mary and O'Shea, Owen, eds. *Kerry, 1916, Histories and Legacies of the Easter Rising – A Centenary Record.* Tralee: Irish Historical Publications, 2016.

McCoole, Sinéad. *No Ordinary Women. Irish Female Activists in the Revolutionary Years 1900-1923.Introduction by Margaret Ward.* Co-published. Madison: University of Wisconsin Press and Dublin: O'Brien Press, 2003.

Mc Hugh, Roger. *Dublin 1916* (London 1966), a miscellany of more than 400 pages.

McHugh, Roger. "The Catholic Church and the Rising", in Owen Dudley Edwards and F. Pyle, eds., *1916: The Easter Rising* (1968).

McKenna, Joseph. *Voices of the Easter Rising: Firsthand Accounts of Ireland's 1916 Rebellion*. Jefferson, NC: McFarland, 2017.

McNally, Michael and David, Peter. *Easter Rising, 1916: Birth of the Irish Republic (Campaign)*. Oxford: Osprey, 2007.

Meeham, Niall. *Sinn Féin Rebellion Handbook*, 1917. pdf.

Nowlan, Kevin B, ed. *The Making of 1916*. Dublin: Stationary Office, 1969.

O Bróin, Léon. *Dublin Castle and the 1916 Rising*, rev.ed. London:Helicon, 1970.

OHogartaigh, Margaret. *Kathleen Lynn, Irishwoman, Patriot, Doctor*. Cheltenham: The History Press, 2006.

O'Malley, Ernie (author) and O'Malley, Corman (editor), *On Another Man's Wound: Ernie O'Malley and Ireland's War for Independence* (Dublin: Mercier Press, 2013).

Rice, Mary Spring. "Diary of the Asgard." Dublin: *An Phoblacht News*. n.d.

Rogers, Rosemary. "Wild Irish Women: Elizabeth O'Farrell—A Fearless Woman." *Irish American Magazine,* February/March 2017.

Ryan, Desmond. *The Rising: The Complete Story of Easter Week Internet Archives: Golden Eagle Reprint*. Internet Archives, 1968.

Schmuhl, Robert. *Ireland's Exiled Children: America and the Easter Rising*. New York: Oxford University Press, 2016.

Shaw, Francis, SJ. "The Canon of Irish History: A Challenge." *Studies*, Vol. LXI (Summer 1972), 113-52.

Sinn Féin Rebellion Handbook. Easter, 1916. Compiled by the *Weekly Irish Times*, Dublin (Fren. Hanna Ltd 1917). 236 pp. with index.

Skinnider, Margaret. *Doing My Bit for Ireland*. London: Louth Press. Kindle ed., 2016.

Stephens, James, *The Insurrection in Dublin.* London and Dublin:Maunsel & Co. Ltd., 1916.

Stedall, Robert. *The Roots of Ireland's Troubles*. South Yorkshire: Pen & Sword Books, 2019.

Taillon, Ruth, *The Women of 1916*. Second edition. Dublin: Tara Press, 2018.

Townshend, Charles. *Easter 1916: The Irish Rebellion*. London: Ivan R. Dee, Reprint Edition, 2011.

Schmuhl, Robert. *Ireland's Exiled Children: American and the Easter Rising*. New York: Oxford University Press. Kindle ed., 2016.

Thompson, W. I., *The Imagination of an Insurrection: Dublin, Easter 1916*. New York: Oxford University Press, 1967.

Ward, Margaret. *Fearless Woman: Hanna Sheehy Skeffington., Feminism and the Irish Revolution*. Chester Springs, IL: Dufour Editions, 2020.

_____*Unmanageable Revolutionaries: Women and Irish Nationalism*. London: Pluto Press, 1995.

Warwick-Haller, Sally, ed. *Letters from Dublin, 1916: Alfred Fannin's Diary of the Rising*. Dublin:IAP, 1995.

Wells, Warre Bradley. *A History of the Irish Rebellion of 1916*. Charleston, SC: Nabu Press. Kindle ed., 2011.

_____ *The Irish Convention and Sinn Fein. In Continuation of "A History of the Irish Rebellion of 1916."* Los Angeles: Hardpress Publishing, 2014.

Williams, Desmond. *The Irish Struggle 1916-1926*. London: RKP, 1966.

Wilson, Scott. *Resting Places: The Burial Sites of More Than 14,000 Famous Persons*. New York: McFarland & Company, 2016.

Zimmerman, Georges-Denis. *Songs of Irish Rebellion: Political Street Ballads and Rebel Songs*. Philadelphia: Folklore Associates, 1967.

MISCELLANEOUS INTERNET SOURCES AND WEBSITES CITED

American Poetry Review archives www.aprweb.org
An Phoblacht https://anphoblacht.com/
BBC News www.bbc.news
BBC History www.bbc.co.uk
Bureau of Military History https://militaryarchives.ie/collections/
online-collections/bureau-of-military-history-1913-1921
The Conversation www.theconversation.com
Finian graves www.finiangraves.net
History Ireland online www.historyireland.com
Independent.ie www.independent.ie
Irish America online www.irishamerica.com
Irish Central www.irishcentral.com
Irish Historical Studies www.irishhistoricalstudies.ie
The Irish Times online www.irishtimes.com
Irish Post online www.irishpost.com
The London Economic www.thelondoneconomic.com
Marxists.org archive www.marxists.org
Military archives (Ireland) online www.militaryacrchives.ie
National College of Arts and Design (Dublin) www.ncad.ie
National Gallery of Ireland www.nationalgallery.ie
New York Times online www.nytimes.com
Radio Teilifís Éireann (RTÉ) online www.rte.com
The Wild Geese https://thewildgeese.irish/
Women's Museum of Ireland online www.womensmuseumofireland.ie
Word Press www.wordpress.org
Royal College of Physicians website www.rcpi.ie

TABLE OF MAPS AND FIGURES

APPENDIX

A. LIST OF KNOWN WOMEN IN THE RISING

Key. Those with a **single asterisk and bold** are ones whose stories are related in the text. Those with a **double asterisk and bold** are widows of the Rising leaders. These women are often omitted from such accounts even though their work in preparation for, during, or in the immediate wake of the Rising (though often behind the scenes) was instrumental.

Adrien, Mary
Allen, Mary
Barrett, Kathleen
Blackburn, Kathleen
Brady, Bridget
Byrne, Katherine
Byrne, Mary
Carron, May
Cavanaugh, Maire
**Ceantt, Áine
*Childers, Molly
Coleton, Elizabeth
**Clarke, Kathleen
**Connolly, Lillie
*Connolly, Nora
Conroy, Eileen
Cooney Harbourne, Eileen
Cooney O'Brien, Ellen
Cooney, Lillie
Costigan, Nellie
Daly, Laura

Daly, Nora
de Barra, Leslie
de Burca, Aoife
Deegan, Maire
Doyle, Mary
English, Maire
Fahy, Anna
Farrell, Rose
*ffrench (sic) Mullen, Madeleine
*Foley, Bridget
Gahan, Mary
Gethings, Lucia
Gifford Donnelly, Helen (Nellie)
Goff Bridget
**Gonne MacBride, Maud
*Grenan, Julia
Greene, Josephine
Hackett, Rosie
Haratty, Emily

Harmon, Bridget
Healy, Cathleen
Hendly, Emily
Heron, Aine
Hoey, Patricia
Hyland, Mary
Jenkinson, Margaret
Joyce, Maggie
Kavanagh, Priscilla
Kealy, Sara
Keating, Pauline
Kelly, Katie
Kelly, May
Kennedy, Margaret
*Keogh, Margaret
Lambert, Bridget
Lane, Kathleen
Lawless, Mary
Lawlor, Mary
Ledwith, Emily
Lynch, Sigle
*Lynn, Kathleen F., Dr.
**MacDonagh (Gifford), Muriel
MacRuaidhu, Sorcha
MacSherry, Margaret
Magee Teresa
Mapotar, Maire
*Markiewicz, Constance (Countess)
Martin, Kathleen
McDubhgaill, Christin Maire
McGavin, Josephine
McGinty, L.
McGuinness, Catherine

McGuinness, Rose
McKean, Brigid,
McLaughlin, Mary
*McNamara, Rose Pat
McNamee, Agnes
McQuaile, May
McSiublaigh, Maire
*Molony, Helena
Moore, May
Morkan, Phyllis
Mulcahy, Mary J.
Murmane, Margaret
Murphy, Gertrude (Gertie)
Murphy, Kathleen
Murphy, Martha
Murphy, Eileen
Murtagh, Frances D.
Ni Brian, Ellis
Ni Conghaile, Brigid
Ni Foghludha, Nora
Ni Rian, Veronia
Noone, Ellen
Norgrove, Annie
O'Brennan, Lily M.
O'Carroll, Annie
O'Carroll, Mary
O'Daly, Bridget
O'Daly, Nora
O'Duffy, Brigid
*O'Farrell, Elizabeth
O'Gorman, Mary Christina
O'Hagan, Annie
O'Hanlon, Mollie
O'Hanrahan, Lily
O'Higgins, Annie

O'Neill Cecilia
O'Reilly, Cathleen
*O'Reilly, Mary (Molly)
Parker Ellen
*Perolz (Flanagan), Marie
**Plunkett (Gifford), Grace
Pollard, Kathleen
Pollard, Louisa
Quigley, Maria
Rafferty, M.J.
Redford, Annie
*Regan, Moira
Reynolds, Mollie
*Rice, Mary Spring
Richard, Birdie
Ryan, Phillis
*Sheehy-Skeffington, Hanna

Simmons, Margaret
*Skinnider, Margaret
Slater, Birdie
Slevin, M.J.
Smith, Lucy
Spicer, Josephine
Stafford, Christina
Stephenson, Mary
Stopford Green, Alice
Stynes, Ellen
Tobin, Annie
Toomey, Stasia
Treston, Cathleen
Ui Conaill, Ellis
Ui Connallain, Peig
Wisely, Esther

Sources: Most of the names were derived from the "Roll of Honor of 1916" prepared by the National Museum of Ireland. I have taken the liberty of adding some names such as those of Margaret Skinnider (Glasgow), Mary Spring Rice (Wales), Molly Childers (Boston), and Moira Regan who fled to the US shortly after the Rising. I have also included the widows of the executed leaders whose names are often omitted but whose contributions should not be forgotten. Finally, I have included Nora Connolly, eldest daughter of James Connolly and founder of the Belfast branch of Cumann na mBan whose efforts were notable in the early stages of the Rising as well as Alice Stopford Green, the Irish historian, whose aid was critical in its inception.

B. FLAGS OF IRELAND, 1916

Fig. 42. The National Flag (The Tricolor).

THE NATIONAL FLAG

The national flag of Ireland is a vertical tricolor of green (next to the staff), white, and orange. It was designed in 1848 and sewn by a group of French women who supported Irish independence. It symbolized the union between Catholics in the south (green) and Protestants in the north (orange) with white in the center standing for peace and solidarity.

In Irish it is called *bratach na Éireann* (national flag) or *an tri-dhathach* (tricolor). It was presented to Thomas Francis Meagher during the Young Ireland Rebellion which occurred in the shadow of the Great Hunger when the potato crop failed, and the English shipped tons of grain out of the country rather than relieve the famine. It brought Protestants and Catholics together in solidarity. Although that rebellion failed, Pádraic Pearse honored the memory of those who fought and reawakened Irish pride when he ordered

Gearóid O'Sullivan to raise the flag again over the GPO during the first day of the Easter Rising.

It was flown during the Irish War of Independence from 1919-21 and later by the Irish Free State. In 1937 it was officially proclaimed the national flag in the new constitution. Since the partition it has been seen by some as a divisive symbol when flown in Northern Ireland by nationalists who reside there. Since it is often flown by the Gaelic Athletic Association, it is sometimes a point of contention at athletic events. The same can be said of the "The Soldiers' Song" which is the Irish National Anthem and has been banned in the North where "God Save the Queen" is mandatory.

Sources: "The Story Behind the Irish Flag," *Irish Central,* Dec. 27, 2020 (https://www.irishcentral.com/roots/history/story-irish-flag, accessed June 12, 2021).

"The Tricolour in Northern Ireland," *Your Irish* (https://web.archive.org/web/20080807173312/http://www.yourirish.com/tricolour-flag.htm, accessed June 12, 2021).

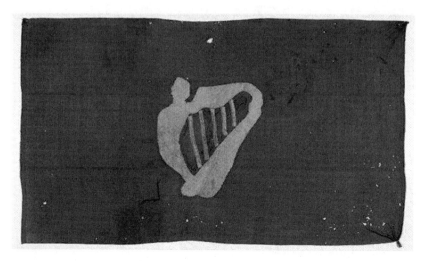

Fig. 43. The Green Flag of Ireland

THE GREEN FLAG

Known as the Green Flag of Ireland, it was raised by the teenager Molly O'Reilly over Liberty Hall the week before the Easter Rising, then again on Easter Monday when the actor and ICA captain, Sean Connolly, raised the flag on the roof of City Hall. He had starred in a play a few weeks before called *Under Which Flag*, a work written by James Connolly (no relation), the Commandant of the Dublin Brigade and military planner of the Rising. The play was about an Irish soldier who found himself conflicted when World War I began and was faced with a choice. Should he join the British forces fighting in Europe as many of his mates were doing? Or should he stay behind and fight for Irish independence? The play ended with the soldier raising the green flag with the golden harp and shouting, "Under this flag only will I serve; under this flag, if need be, I will die."

The origins of the flag can be traced back to France when the Brigade Irlandaise fought for that country. It was a group composed of Irish warriors (known as the "Wild Geese") who left Ireland for

France after the ascension of William of Orange and had a green regimental banner. The uncle of "The Liberator" Daniel O'Connell was a general in this regiment. The golden harp device was part of the flag presented to the regiment called "the Farewell Banner" when they left the French Army in 1792 after the declaration of the French Republic. In 1798 a green flag with a golden harp was carried in the Irish Rebellion that year, and again in the rebellion of 1803. The harp with the female head evolved over time.

The flag was also carried by the Fenians and by the forces of the independence movements led by Daniel O'Connor in the 1830s and 1840s.

Source: Robert Lee, *The Green Flag: A History of Irish Nationalism.* New York: Penguin, 2000.

Fig. 44. Remnants of the Irish Republic Flag which was raised over the GPO.

IRISH REPUBLIC FLAG

This is a green flag which hung from the flagpole closest to the Prince's Street side of the GPO roof during the Easter Rising. The original still exists today and is part of an exhibition at the National Museum of Ireland. It is made of wool and the letters are painted white and orange with house paint in letters that read: "Irish Republic." The flag was designed by Countess Markiewicz and painted in her home at Rathmines by Theobald Fitzgerald.

The flag was raised by Harry Walpole and Séan Hegarty on orders from James Connolly on Easter Monday. On Friday of Easter Week, the flagpole was shattered, the flag fell, and was captured by British soldiers. It was taken as a trophy and exhibited at the Imperial Museum in London for the next 50 years. In 1966 it was returned to Ireland. Both it and the "Tricolor" (of which only fragments remain) show marks from bullets and from the GPO fires.

Sources: Statement of Harry Walpole, 1949. Bureau of Military History.

National Museum of Ireland, Research Collections (https://www.museum.ie/en-IE/Collections-Research/Collection/Resilience/Artefact/Test-4/8961f46b-5885-4aea-af9d-63894e2b76b4, accessed June 12, 2021).

Fig. 45. Original design of the Starry Plough Flag (1914). Wikimedia Commons. Public domain.

THE STARRY PLOUGH FLAG

The official flag of the Irish Citizen's Army was commonly known as the Starry Plough. It featured a green background with a golden plough utilizing a sword as the ploughshare. There were also five white stars (silver in the original) symbolizing Ursa Major ("The Great Bear"), known as "The Big Dipper" in the US, but as "The Plough" in Britain and Ireland.

The theme of the sword and the plough alludes to a biblical verse: "They will beat their swords into plowshares and their spears into pruning hooks. Nation will not rise up against nation, nor will they train for war anymore" (Isaiah 2:4). The flag flew across from the GPO on the roof of the Imperial Hotel on Sackville Street during the Easter Rising.

This first Starry Plough differed somewhat from the version currently used by, among others, the Sinn Fein, the IRA and the Irish Labour Party. Some groups have utilized a blue version of the original, similar to the state flag of Alaska which it predates by several years. The Alaska flag creator chose the design to include the Great Bear reference since the bear is indigenous to that state. The identity of the designer of the original version is still a source of dispute. It is generally accepted that the streamlining of the design was carried out by William Megahy, a teacher at the Metropolitan School of Arts in Dublin. Others contend that George W. Russell first proposed the design. To this day it remains unclear precisely who conceived the Starry Plough. An ICA banner was first proposed when the ICA was simply a worker's defense force formed after the brutality of attacks on the Dublin workers in 1913. However, when James Larkin, the founder, left the organization for the US in October 1814, new leader James Connolly conceived of it as a revolutionary organization dedicated to the creation of an Irish socialist republic. Connolly said that the banner symbolized that a free Ireland would control its destiny from the plough to the stars and be an inspiration to the world.

In 1926 Sean O'Casey wrote a play called *The Plough and the Stars* which was about the Irish Rising and the differences between the ideals of some and the gross indifference of others. In Act II rebel soldiers come into a public house (where a prostitute has complained that the revolutionaries were bad for business), carrying both the Tricolor and the Plough and Stars. The packed audience at the Abbey Theatre, many of whom were members of the IRA and the Cumann na mBan, began to boo and shout, feeling that the flag was being disrespected. It led to a riot which was only quelled when William Butler Yeats, who was highly respected and an icon, addressed the crowd. The flag had achieved sacred status.

Source: "History of the Starry Plough Flag,"IRSP Derry website (https://www.angelfire.com/space/derryirsp/flaghistory.htm, accessed June 12, 2021).

Fig. 46. Modern version of the Starry Plough flag which infers the connection between the plough and the stars and forms a visual metaphor rather than the 1914 visual simile.

C. PLAYS, POEMS AND SONGS OF THE RISING.

I have not gathered gold;
The fame that I won perished;
In love I found but sorrow,
That withered my life.

Of wealth or of glory
I shall leave nothing behind me
(I think it, O God, enough!)
But my name in the heart of a child.

Pádraic Pearse

This is a personal section, written as a teacher, to share with my students in Latin American and the US who do not know much about the cultural forces that surrounded the Rising and how they played a role and/or provided an ambient background. I want to give them a sense of what the music was like at the time, and what poems and dramatic performances preceded or followed. This poem quoted above was written by Pearse shortly before his death. His hope to be remembered by his students is, of course, shared by many teachers, even though we also know that we are mere conduits. As my grandfather used to remind me, "The story outlives the teller, bucko, and is always finer."

Plays. It is important to remember that, before Lady Augusta Gregory and William Butler Yeats founded the Abbey Theatre, there was no national Irish theater or venue for Irish playwrights. The plays that were performed in the theaters were mostly social comedies and drawing-room dramas featuring upper-class English characters and appealing to well-to-do audiences. First as a group called the Irish Literary Theatre, then as the Irish National Theater Company, Yeats, Gregory and Frank Fay attracted excellent local talent, including the very beautiful and talented Maud Gonne who played to packed houses. The plays were gritty, often featuring working men and women, who spoke in the language of the street. Some of the plays were overtly political and provocative.

The most famous (or notorious) of these was *Cathleen Ni Houlihan*. The play is set in a family cottage in County Mayo. Michael, one of the sons, is to marry Delia the next day. Michael enters the cottage with Delia's dowry in a bag to the delight of his parents. Shortly thereafter, a mysterious Old Woman knocks on the cottage door, and they invite her in. The Old Woman tells how she was evicted from her home, and how far she has traveled. Her reason for wandering is the fact that there are "too many strangers" in her house, and that they have usurped her home and her "four green fields" (symbolizing the ancient provinces of Ireland). The Old Woman begins singing verses of Gaelic songs, about a young man who sacrificed himself for loving her. The parents try to offer her some money for her troubles, but she refuses, and tells them she needs people to give themselves completely to her and her cause. When she goes to leave, Michael wants to accompany her, forgetting about his marriage to Delia. The Old Woman then reveals herself to be Cathleen Ni Houlihan and she exits the stage.

As the mother tries to snap her son out of his hypnotic state, his brother Patrick and fiancée Delia come into the cottage. Michael, who is still under the enchantment of Cathleen Ni Houlihan, rushes outside to follow her and fight for the cause of Irish independence and nationalism. The family is frantic and they ask Patrick if he has crossed paths with an old woman on his way home. Patrick says he only saw a young girl with "the walk of a queen."

It is often credited as one of the literary works that led to the Rising. Many of those who fought were in fact young men and women who had either acted in the play or been in the audience. Later in a poem Yeats would write:

I lie awake night after night
And never get the answers right.
Did that play of mine send out
Certain men the English shot?
Did words of mine put too great strain
On that woman's reeling brain?
Could my spoken words have checked
That whereby a house lay wrecked?
And all seems evil until I
Sleepless would lie down and die.

("The Man and the Echo")

Under Which Flag has already been discussed as an even closer connection. Written by James Connolly, starring Sean Connolly, both men were certainly inspired by the play or found in it a further spur to their already galloping nationalism. Sean Connolly would actually be shot while attempting to raise the exact same flag he carried on the stage (see "The Green Flag", Appendix B).

Many of those who later participated in the Rising either acted, wrote, or worked as ushers or stagehands at the Theatre. Beside the two Connollys, there was also Thomas MacDonagh, poet and playwright; Nora Desmond, Helena Molony and Constance Markiewicz who acted; Pádraic Pearse, who also wrote plays; and many of his boys from St. Enda's School who worked at a number of tasks both in front of and behind the curtains.

Poems. There are dozens of poems written about the Rising. Perhaps the most famous and most quoted is Yeats' "Easter, 1916." All of his poems are now in the public domain (as of 2010) so they can be copied and used in a variety of educational motifs.

...That woman's days were spent
In ignorant good will,
Her nights in argument
Until her voice grew shrill.   CONSTANCE MARKIEWICZ
What voice more sweet than hers
When young and beautiful,
She rode to harriers?
This man had kept a school
And rode our winged horse.   PÁDRAIC PEARSE
This other his helper and friend
Was coming into his force;
He might have won fame in the end,   THOMAS MACDONAGH
So sensitive his nature seemed,
So daring and sweet his thought.
This other man I had dreamed
A drunken, vain-glorious lout.   JOHN MACBRIDE
                                      (MARRIED TO MAUD GONNE)
He had done most bitter wrong   WHO WAS YEATS'
                                           UNREQUITED LOVE.

To some who are near my heart,
Yet I number him in the song;
He, too, has resigned his part
In the casual comedy;
He, too, has been changed in his turn,
Transformed utterly:
A terrible beauty is born....

We know their dream; enough
To know they dreamed and are dead.
And what if excess of love
Bewildered them till they died?
I write it out in a verse —
MacDonagh and MacBride
And Connolly and Pearse
Now and in time to be,

Wherever green is worn,
Are changed, changed utterly:
A terrible beauty is born.

MacDonagh, the poet "who might have won fame in the end," is little known and his poetry is uneven. He is best remembered by a short verse of Francis Ledwidge, a World War I poet who wrote

"Lament for Thomas MacDonagh."
He shall not hear the bittern cry
In the wild sky where he is lain
Nor voices of the sweeter birds
Above the wailing of the rain.

Ledwidge did not long outlive his friend. He was killed in action on July 30, 1917, at the Battle of Passchendaele.

Other poems of passing interest to the reader but of mixed quality include

"The Rose Tree" by W.B. Yeats
"Sixteen Dead Men" by W.B. Yeats
"An Irish Airman Foresee his Death" by W.B. Yeats
"September 1913 by John O'Leary
"The Spring in Ireland" by James Stephens
"Easter Week" by Joyce Kilmer
"The Mother" by Pádraic Pearse
"I see His Blood Upon the Rose" by Joseph Plunkett
"The Foggy Dew" by Canon Charles O'Neill
"The Wayfarer" by Patrick Pearse
"Connolly" by Liam MacGabhann
"Wishes for my Son" by Thomas MacDonagh
"Comrades" by Eva Gore-Booth

SONGS. "The Soldier's Song" is the Irish National Anthem. The lyrics were composed by Peadar Kearney in English and the music by his friend and neighbor Patrick Heeney back in 1909. The Irish verse which we hear today at most official events is a translation by Liam O'Rinn. The English version is the original and was published in flysheets (handbills) for a ha'penny. It was sung by the rebels in the GPO as well as in the Kilmainham Gaol and in the internment camps after the Rising. Most knew the first verse and chorus by heart.

We'll sing a song, a soldier's song,
With cheering rousing chorus,
As round our blazing fires we throng,
The starry heavens o'er us;
Impatient for the coming fight,
And as we wait the morning's light,
Here in the silence of the night,
We'll chant a soldier's song.

CHORUS
Soldiers are we
whose lives are pledged to Ireland;
Some have come
from a land beyond the wave.
Sworn to be free,
No more our ancient sire land
Shall shelter the despot or the slave.

There were many popular songs of the day which were widely known and played at home with instruments and sheet music or fly sheets. A few rebels from more comfortable circumstances had a Victrola gramophone and could hear the recording artists of the day singing them. Some of the hits in 1916 by sales of gramophone wax cylinders are listed below. The most popular Irish singer for the day and for many decades thereafter was John McCormack.

Here are some of the songs and the dates recorded. A few were both written and recorded earlier, for example, "Beautiful Isle of Somewhere," but it is the McCormack recording which reached the top of the charts.

"Somewhere a Voice is Calling" (1914)
"Beautiful Isle of Somewhere" (1915)
"A Long, long Way to Tipperary" (1915)
"My Wild Irish Rose" (1915)
"A Little Bit of Heaven" (1916)

Some of the songs which memorialized Irish rebellions both before and after the Rising are listed below:

"The Boys of the Old Brigade" (1881)
"Mise Erie" ("I am Ireland") (1912)
"Foggy Dew" (1919
"The West's Asleep" (1844)
"Banna Strand" (1966)
"Off to Dublin in the Green" (1966)
"The Ballad of James Connolly" (1968)
"Grace" (1985)
"Wearing of the Green" (1841)

There are many more, of course, but this is a fair sampling.

Lest one underestimate the power of music and personal accounts, it is interesting to note that the popularity of "Wearing of the Green" increased dramatically when sung by McCormack after Nora Connolly's visit to Boston in July of 1916 during which she vividly described the brutal death of her father. A week later, Hanna Sheehy-Skeffington spoke of the murder of her husband by a deranged British officer and how it was covered up by the British.

While the government of Woodrow Wilson was reluctant to condemn the British then fighting in World War I, the American public was not so reticent. Moreover, they put their money behind their sympathy and donated generously to the Sinn Fein and the Republican causes as well as to a fund for the relief of the widows of the Rising leaders. The Irish Relief Fund in Boston raised $2,330 in one night at Boston Symphony Hall. The National Volunteers of Ireland held a fundraiser in Roxbury. A letter was read from Eoin MacNeill, chairman of the provisional committee in Dublin, stating that "arms were badly needed," and asking the Irish in Boston to rise to the occasion. Friends of Irish Freedom leader Joseph Smith of Lowell traveled to Ireland with $100,000. By August, the Irish Relief Fund had raised an additional £100,000 for the widows and orphans of the Rising's leaders. Rather than ending the Irish revolt, the actions of the English revitalized it and brought them more allies in their struggle for independence.

I met with Napper Tandy, and he took me by the hand
And he said, "How's poor old Ireland and how does she stand?"
"She's the most distressful country that ever yet was seen
For they're hanging men and women there for Wearing of the Green."
Then since the color we must wear is England's cruel red
Sure Ireland's sons will never forget the blood that they have shed
You may pull the shamrock from your hat and cast it on the sod
But 'twill take root and flourish there, though underfoot 'tis trod.
When laws can stop the blades of grass for growing as they grow
And when the leaves in summertime their verdure dare not show
Then I will change the color too I wear in my caubeen
But 'til that day, please God, I'll stick to Wearing of the Green.
But if at last our color should be torn from Ireland's heart
Her sons, with shame and sorrow, from the dear old Isle will part
I've heard a whisper of a land that lies beyond the seaWhere rich and poor stand equal in the light of Freedom's day.
Ah, Erin, must we leave you, driven by a tyrant's hand
Must we seek a mother's blessing from a strange and distant land

Where the cruel cross of England shall never more be seen
And where, please God, we'll live and die, still Wearing of the
Green.

South Boston, a neighborhood that was home to a robust Irish community, was also the site of Dorchester Heights, where the evacuation of British troops from Boston on March 17, 1776, during the
American Revolution is commemorated. Given the significance of
both the St. Patrick's Day and Evacuation Day holidays, the parade
came to honor both. And everyone who attended, regardless of
their ancestry, wore a bit of green to signify solidarity with the Irish
and their love of freedom. It was due in no small part to this show
of solidarity that the British were forced to the bargaining table in
1921 to concede the first measures of Irish independence.

Sources

"Top Hit songs in US and UK, 1916", *Playback.FM*
(https://playback.fm/charts/top-100-songs/1916,
accessed June 2, 2021).

Michael Quinlin, "Boston and the Irish Rising", *Irish American
Magazine*, Feb.-Mar. 2016 (https://irishamerica.com/2016/02/bos-
ton-and-the-irish-rising/, accessed June 2, 2021).

Poetry of W.B. Yeats. Public domain.
Song lyrics. Public domain.

AUTHOR BIOGRAPHY

Michael Hogan is the author of 26 books, including the best-selling *Irish Soldiers of Mexico* which has been the basis of an MGM movie and three documentaries. He is Emeritus Humanities Chair at the American School Foundation of Guadalajara, and a former professor of International Relations at the Autonomous University of Guadalajara. He is a member of the Organization of American Historians, the International Association of Military History, and the Society of Geography and Statistics in Mexico. Dr. Hogan is a second-generation Irish American with roots in both County Kerry and County Clare and has travelled extensively in Ireland with the Mexican Embassy promoting Irish-Mexican solidarity and shared traditions.

Please visit the author's page at http://www.drmichaelhogan.com

OTHER BOOKS BY MICHAEL HOGAN

HISTORY AND HISTORICAL FICTION

Guns Grit and Glory: How the US and Mexico Came Together to Defeat the Last Empire in the Americas, 2019

Abraham Lincoln and Mexico: A History of Courage, Intrigue and Unlikely Friendships, 2016

Abraham Lincoln y México: Un Relato de Valentía, Intriga y Amistades Improbables, Spanish Edition, 2016

The Irish Soldiers of Mexico, 2011

Los Soldados Irlandeses de México, Spanish Edition, 2012

Molly Malone and the San Patricios, 2011

Molly Malone Y Los San Patricios, Spanish Edition, 2012

ESSAYS AND OTHER NON-FICTION

Living Is No Laughing Matter, A Primer on Existential Optimism, 2020

Newport: A Writer's Beginnings, 2012

Teaching from the Heart: Essays and Speeches on Teaching at American Schools in Latin America, 2011

Intelligent Mistakes, 2011

Twelve Habits of the Creative Mind, 2011

A Writer's Manual For Inmates in Correctional Institutions, 2011

Savage Capitalism and the Myth of Democracy, 2009

Mexican Mornings, 2006

POETRY

In the Time of the Jacarandas, 2015
Winter Solstice, 2012
Imperfect Geographies, 2011
Making Our Own Rules: New and Selected Poems, 1989
The broken face of summer: Poems, 1981
Rust, 1977
Risky Business, 1977
Soon it will be morning, 1976
Letters For My Son, 1975

FICTION

A Metaphorical Piano and Other Stories, 2013
A Lion at a Cocktail Party, 35th Anniversary Edition, 2013
A Death in Newport, 2011

ACKNOWLEDGEMENTS

The author and publisher wish to thank the following people who have read and commented on early drafts of this book for their time, critical analyses, and helpful comments. A special note of gratitude to the scholars at *Academia.com* who read selected portions for peer review prior to recommending for publication. We are especially grateful to the readers from *Ireland*: Pat McDermott, Fiachra Keogh, Vincent Brown of the University of Dublin, and Professor Lauren Addington, National University of Ireland, Maynooth; from *Mexico*: friend and editor Mikel Miller; students Maria Fernanda Barragán and Elfriede Suarez Richenberger, and AP Capstone teacher Alicja Surzyn, all from the American School Foundation of Guadalajara, and Lina Hall from Mexico City; from the *United States*: Professor Robert DiYanni of New York University, Cliff Carlson, publisher of Irish American News, Erika Moore, Vice President of North America Travel Solutions (Sabre), Ciara Archer, director of the Irish Cultural Center and the McClellan Library; and Ken Youngblood, Emeritus Humanities Professor, State University of New York; from the *UK*, Dr Hugh Goodacre, Professor of Economics, University College London, and from *Argentina*: Profesora María Eugenia Cruset, Universidad de la Plata (Buenos Aires).

Finally, a warm thanks to Hannah Wilkes, line editor and proofreader, for her meticulous work, her patience, and enthusiasm for this project.

INDEX KEY WORDS

Made in the USA
Middletown, DE
08 February 2022

60586899R00163